**A STORY OF FATHERHOOD,
FATE AND FORGIVENESS**

And Then We Went Fishing

Dirk Benedict

AVERY PUBLISHING GROUP INC.

Garden City Park, New York

Cover Design: Ann Vestal and Ed Foster
Cover Photo: Joan Lauren, Los Angeles, CA
In-House Editors: Marie Caratozzolo and Barbara Conner
Typesetter: Bonnie Freid

The following exerpts have been reprinted with permission:

"WINTER WONDERLAND"
(Felix Bernard, Dick Smith)
© 1934 (Renewed) WB MUSIC CORP.
All Rights Reserved.   Used By Permission
(Exerpt found on page 138)

The Decline of the West, Volume II, by Oswald Spengler
Published in 1928 by Alfred A. Knopf, Inc.
(Exerpt found on prematter quotation page)

Library of Congress Cataloging-in-Publication Data

Benedict, Dirk.
    And then we went fishing ; a story of fatherhood, fate, and
forgiveness / Dirk Benedict.
        p.   cm.
    ISBN 0-89529-559-8

    1. Benedict, Dirk.   2. Benedict, Dirk—Family.   3. Actors—
United States—Biography.   I. Title.

RN2287.B427A3   1993
791.45'028'092—dc20   93-15107
                                                           [B] CIP

Printed in the United States of America

10 9 8 7 6 5 4 3 2 1

To My Mother, My Brother, My Sister,
On the 30th Anniversary
Of that of which we never . . .
Speak.

In the hope that we may all, finally and forever,
bury the dead, let the living live, and forgive
ourselves that which needs no forgiveness.

. . . the beast knows only life, not death. Were we pure plantlike beings, we should die unconscious of dying, for to feel death and to die would be identical. But animals, even though they hear the death-cry, see the dead body, and scent putrefaction, behold death without comprehending it. Only when understanding has become, through language, detached from visual awareness and pure, does death appear to man as the great enigma of the light-world about him.

Then, and only then, life becomes the short span of time between birth and death . . . only then does the diffuse animal fear of everything become the definite human fear of death. It is this that makes the love of man and woman, the love of mother and child, the tree of the generations, the family, the people, and so at last world-history itself, the infinitely deep facts and problems of destiny that they are. . . . In the knowledge of death is originated that world-outlook which we possess as being men and not beasts.

The Decline of the West
Oswald Spengler

A man writes to throw off the poison which he has accumulated because of his false way of life. He is trying to recapture his innocence. . . .

Sexus
Henry Miller

Prologue

I t is a hard thing to learn that reality is relative. That one person's red is another's orange. That one child's pain is another's joy. That what is true for me is false for another. The following story is true. For me. As God knows, there are others who could also tell this story. I cannot and do not speak for them. They must speak for themselves. What is essential to remember, and even more difficult to learn, is that there is a spiritual truth to all our lives and the stories they contain, and that that spiritual truth is absolute and does not change no matter who tells the story. The colors, emotions, thoughts, and feelings of this tale, then, are mine. They may or may not be true for others. But their spirit and the spirit of this story are the absolute truth.

It is essentially two stories told as one. The birth of my first child and the death of my father. Shortly after our child was born, my wife insisted that I sit down, while the experience was still fresh in my mind, and write the story. I did so. My father died thirty years ago. Were it a hundred, I could never forget who said what to whom and when. I can, therefore, attest to the veracity of all the words uttered by those involved in both stories. The quotation marks don't come easy.

During the thirty years since my father's death, I have tried once a decade to put it all on paper. But it was always too soon, too impossible, and beyond me. This, my fourth attempt to tell that story, was made possible by my wife, Toni, and the experience we had with the birth of our first child.

There's always the danger, as any politician will tell you, that when you write something down on paper, it will fall into the wrong hands and get published. Writing a book, I have discovered, is a kind of birth, and the book becomes its own reality apart and separate from its creator. Such has been the case. And as much as I, creator of this wayward child, have resisted its desire to go into public life, it has been to no avail. It has fallen into the wrong hands of those who feel it has some value in easing the pain of others who may also have tasted some of the bitter pills of youth that I was forced to swallow. Such was not my intention, but there has been nothing I can do to convince this literary offspring of mine that it was not meant to be read by strangers. It will do, as children will, what it damn well pleases. I can only hope that it is accepted for what it is, one man's little story of his rise from the ashes of enormous pain, and that it causes no further pain to anyone who reads its pages, but brings instead some new appreciation for birth, death, and the miracle of love that surrounds them.

Chapter One

I am forty-five miles out of town, forty-three years into life, two years into marriage, one hundred pages into my first screenplay, and nine months into the pregnancy of my first child. I think I have arrived. Little do I know what a long, long way I have to go.

Before there can be birth, I will have to face death. Not mine, of course. I have already done that in the form of prostate cancer. That was easy. Wrote a book to tell the world just how easy it was. And now the screenplay I write will share that journey with those carcinogenic millions who have forgotten how to read.

The screenplay, the marriage, the impending state of fatherhood are all new adventures. Reflections of a man realizing his deepest dreams. Facing his worst nightmares. Without knowing it. (Which is the only way.) We are only capable of living up to that finest part of ourselves, facing that darkest truth about ourselves, if we are thrust into it.

The place is Agua Dulce, California. The date, February 26, 1988. The weather is cold, wet, windy, and wonderful. I love Mother Nature best when she is at her worst. She and I are having a mad love affair this last February weekend during the final weeks, days, moments of my wife's pregnancy with our first child. The rain, wind, and lightning have been going on for some days and are what I consider the perfect climate for the reincarnation of the kind of soul I pray will choose me as its father. After all, my life has been nothing if not an acceptance of the maxim that it is always out of the storms of life that we receive our greatest periods of growth. Those experiences we are taught to avoid (misfortune, failure, sickness, sorrow) are the very things that test us, shape us, reveal us. Let the babe be born into the eye of the tempest. Give him or her, a taste for wildness. As Henry David Thoreau once said, "In wildness is the preservation of the world." And yet, knowing this, I would have retreated from the experience I am about to have as I sit cozily in my study and hammer out the final scenes of my first screenplay. I would have avoided the birth of my son just as I would have avoided the death of my Father. Had I only known. . . .

In 1963, I was eighteen years old. Going on fifty. My Father was fifty-one. Teetering on the brink of eternity. Or oblivion if you are a non-believer. My journey out of the small town of White Sulphur Springs, Montana, (population 1,000) was about to begin. His journey through life was about to end. I tingled with anticipation. He despaired with the dread that comes of knowing you have failed in that part of your life where it matters most . . . with your family. My childhood had been rich in all the ways that only life in a small town can be. My "entertainment" had been Mother Nature. She was my church, my psychiatrist, my best friend . . . my savior. I walked her mountains, streams, and valleys. Hunted, fished, and languished by her cold, crystal-clear mountain lakes as I dealt with all the pains of growing up that any boy encounters and a few that none should ever have to.

My Sister was fifteen. The youngest child and only daughter in a family ruled by men. She loved horses, playing the French horn, and, in a family of carnivores and hunters, abhorred the taste of meat and cried at the sight of road kill. Hers was not the stomach for the emotional day-to-day warfare and eventual physical carnage of the family into which she was born. A sensitive girl with a loving nature and a natural gift for cheer-leading, she found few cheers to lead in the house she called home. So she rode her horse in summers of silence, led winter cheers for her high school heroes, and kept her fears within.

My Brother was twenty-four, an early riser and an avid hunter. He loaded all his own ammunition for a bolt-action .243 Winchester Savage and was a very good shot.

My Brother, my Father and I had grown up hunting together. But never each other. Or had we? Don't all sons stalk their fathers? Isn't patricide something we all have practiced to some extent as part of our maturation? Is it not essential, if they are ever truly going to pass into manhood, that all sons kill their fathers' hold on them? To become their own men in preparation for their own transition into fatherhood and their sons' need to be rid of them. And on and on, generation after generation. Throughout history, certain cultures have had very extensive rituals for this all-important passage into manhood. None of which included pulling the trigger of a big-game rifle. But sometimes, when all else fails and the child is suffocating and desperate, and the technology is at hand. . . .

When it comes to hunting big game, there is none bigger than one's own father.

As I work passionately to finish my screenplay, and the wind and rain lash at my Agua Dulce window and clouds scuttle across a full moon, I hear the sound of the .243 Winchester Savage. The sound of my Father's passing, of my Brother's silence, my Mother's and Sister's terror. All the sounds of the worst day of my life filter through my mind's eye and ear on these final few days before what I know is to be the best day of my life with the birth of my first child.

But this is 1988 and I don't want the sounds, the memories of 1963. I am determined, as I have been for the past twenty-five years, not to deal with this now. For now I want only the vision of life, not the memory of death. I force my mind to focus not on the death of my Father, but on the birth of my baby.

When my first and only wife, Toni, informed me we had been chosen by a soul to be its parents, we decided we would have our baby the old-fashioned way and accept the responsibility for that soul's delivery into this life. Our child would be born at home with only a midwife to assist us. The midwife would share her experience and knowledge, but the responsibility for the quality of the birth would be directly in the hands of Toni and me. Every aspect of this home birth would be a reflection of how we lived our lives. We would face the truth about ourselves. It would be a learning experience. Little did I know just how much I had to learn.

My Father's ghost had been following me for the twenty-five years since his death. How can I not know that? There is no denial as strong as that which we have for our parents. It wasn't only my Father's body that was lowered into the grave on that beautiful summer afternoon at the Castle Mountain Cemetery in White Sulphur Springs, Montana, in August 1963. When my brother's finger squeezed the trigger of the .243 Savage, I knew I had been wounded. What I didn't know was that I had died. In that fraction of an instant, which seemed then and now to last an eternity, a part of me, the *essential* part, died.

They say that when a person loses a leg or an arm, for a long time he still feels the presence of the missing limb. In his mind it is still there and he will reach with the missing arm to pick up a cup. It is only when the cup doesn't get picked up, only in the failure to accomplish what his heart and mind wish to do, that he realizes he is no longer in possession of the missing limb. And so it was with me. Only it wasn't an arm or a leg that was missing. It was *me*! And for twenty-five years, when I reached out to move the cups in my life and they didn't move, it took great powers of rationalization to pretend that they did move. Or were not really worth moving in the first place because they were empty or held within them that which I didn't really want or was not meant to have or *didn't deserve* to have.

I had total plegia and didn't know it. Like the recent amputee, I was functioning as if I still had all my parts. It would be necessary for me to rob my Father's grave to recover my lost Self.

Chapter Two

Friday, February 26, 1988. The birth of our baby is imminent. Nine days overdue according to the experts. But who listens to them? Certainly not me. Because most women do not know when conception took place (some aren't even sure with whom), doctors use the date of a woman's last menstrual cycle as the basis for predicting the birth date. My wife, being a responsible woman, knew exactly when our child was conceived . . . June 1st. And where . . . in the Bahama Islands. And with whom . . . me. By my calculations, March 1 is the date this soul will be born. You figure it out.

One thing is certain, overdue or right on schedule, our baby is very, very close to his planetary entrance. Knowing this, I've spent this Friday rushing to finish the screenplay of my first book, *Confessions of a Kamikaze Cowboy*, because I suspect that after the birth I might be more interested in the new soul in our presence than in something as mundane as writing.

I started writing at 6:00 in the morning. At 6:00 in the evening, Toni brings dinner to my writing cubicle. We hug and kiss good night with a tenderness that is unique for a husband and wife on the brink of parenthood, then she goes to bed. I keep working in a mad rush to finish. At 11:00, exhausted, I type "The End" and collapse beside Toni in the bed that is to be our delivery table.

At 1:30 in the morning, a gentle nudge brings me out of my sleep. Toni tells me she has been having contractions since midnight. Uh oh. This could be it. The thought of waking up, let alone starting the process of having our baby, is over-whelming. The climb out of bed is a climb from the grave. I'm not sure I can make it. Maybe this is a false alarm? Maybe the contractions will go away and I can blissfully slide back under the warm covers and sleep? Find out how far apart the contractions are. This will give us an idea of just how far along we are in this process. Three minutes? I can't believe it. The contractions are just three minutes apart. This is very strange.

I have done my homework, taken classes. I know, in theory, how this is *supposed* to go. Early Labor begins with contractions that last about thirty seconds and are from ten to thirty minutes apart. Not *three minutes*! This isn't supposed to happen till Middle Labor. Then comes the Transition, where contractions are about a minute and a half in length with only one minute in between. Transition is the roughest, most intense stage of labor and usually requires a lot of coaching because it is important that the woman does not begin to push during this phase, although the urge to do so is very strong.

Pushing is forbidden because the mother's cervix is not fully dilated; so to push would be premature, as pushing is the action that moves the baby down the birth canal towards Expulsion, which is impossible until the mother is fully dilated.

You see how complicated this gets? A woman's cervix needs to be dilated ten centimeters before the baby can be born. The first three centimeters of dilation take place during Early Labor; Middle Labor, three to seven centimeters; and the final three centimeters of dilation occur during Transition. *Then* a woman begins all that pushing you see in the movies, and if all goes according to God's plan, the baby is born. So I know timing contractions is a good way to find out how far along you are in the process of having your child. According to my trusty stopwatch, Toni is in Middle Labor and well on her way. She must have slept through the contractions of Early Labor. I do some quick calculating. In ten to twelve hours we should have our little baby in our arms. Do I have the endurance, I wonder? Toni I'm not worried about; she's dealing with each contraction the same way she deals with life. Steady and calm, taking each moment as it comes. Me? I'm a different story. As we shall soon see.

I talk to myself. "Okay, we're in Middle Labor. Never mind, Toni and I have been studying, preparing for this home birth for months. We are ready. I have done months of research. I understand the process. I know what to expect and when. Hell, I've grown up on ranches. Seen all kinds of farm animals born. Helped in their delivery. I can handle this."

Decades ago I starred on Broadway in *Butterflies Are Free*. The butterflies I had in my stomach on opening night were nothing compared to what I now feel fluttering, but what the hell . . . this is the experience of a lifetime. Look at it as an adventure.

An adventure into an unknown future. Into a past I've tried to forget.

Chapter Three

I've heard a lot of gunfire in my life. Not just the Hollywood variety with blanks and mock death and glamorized violence, but the real stuff. Up close and personal. Guns don't frighten me. I understand them. They have taught me many things: that there is more to killing than pulling the trigger; that you don't have to be shot to be wounded. I know what guns can do, not to the dead, for that is easy and obvious, but to the living. Guns can be your best friend or your worst enemy. They've been both to me. Oh, yes.

To grow up in Montana is to grow up with guns. Shortly after you learn how to handle a knife and fork, you learn how to handle a gun. My family was no exception. Except, as in all things, my Father had very stringent rules as to how a gun should be handled. You never point a gun at another person. This may sound like an obvious rule, but when you are hunting deer or ducks or pheasants or elk with four or five other people, it isn't unusual for the barrel of a rifle to swing casually, though briefly, in the direction of one of your hunting partners. With my Father it was an unforgivable sin. To walk in the midst of a hunting party as it moves through a field or forest and *never* let the muzzle of your weapon point toward a member of that party requires great skill and practice. One must constantly shift and move the rifle in the fashion of a highly skilled military drill team. Our Father also went to great lengths to instill in my Brother and me the proper technique for crossing a fence when carrying a rifle: You set the rifle down or, if you were with someone else, you handed it to that person *before* crossing the fence. You were then handed the rifle after you crossed or, if you were hunting alone, reached back for it after you crossed.

I was hunting alone. I was twelve years old and in a very big hurry. Who would know that I was climbing through the barbed-wire fence with my 12-gauge Ithaca Featherweight shotgun firmly in my grasp? Certainly not my Father. Anyway, the gun wasn't loaded! What could be the harm? My Father always said that it is the unloaded gun that kills, that "ignorance is no excuse." That "Gee, I didn't know the gun was loaded" may assuage your remorse, but it would never stand up in a court of law. But I was twelve, in a very big hurry, and had no time for fatherly advice.

It was a cold, late afternoon in November. I knew there was a bunch of sage hens hanging out in the hayfields in back of town. I had been walking for about an hour to get there before it got dark and was in the kind of hurry you are always in when you're twelve and don't realize you have the rest of your life to get there. Or that if you don't get "there," it not only doesn't matter, you probably weren't meant to get there in the first place.

As I reached the fence surrounding the hayfield, I could see the bobbing heads of the sage hens feeding in the field. My heart began to pound. I knew what I was doing, and not doing, as I climbed through the barbed-wire fence, my 12-gauge shotgun clasped firmly in the hands of innocence. And ignorance.

I lay in the snow where the muzzle blast had knocked me and watched sage hens whir out of the hayfield, set their wings, and glide beneath the gray, overcast November sky. The roar of the 12-gauge came echoing back to me from very far away. If not my life, my hunting trip was over.

To this day, I have 50 percent hearing loss in my left ear, where, even on the warmest of days, I can still "feel" the cold steel of the 12-gauge Ithaca.

The powder burns and blood took some explaining. Some lying. Only I would know what really happened. Sitting in my eighth-grade class listening to the teacher, my whole body would begin to shake as the full impact of what didn't happen would finally sink in. Why didn't the shotgun take my twelve-year-old head off as it exploded halfway through the barbed-wire fence and inches from my face? Why did I lose only my hearing and not my life? Fate? Destiny? Luck?

How easily it all could have ended on that cold November afternoon. I didn't and I don't understand how the shotgun came to have a shell in the chamber with its safety off. It's still a mystery to me. One that I gave up trying to solve long ago.

But every time I have to turn my head to hear a conversation or lay my good ear down on my pillow to shut out the city noise so I can sleep, I remember my Father's words: "It is always the *unloaded* gun that kills us." For truly there is no such thing. All guns, all experiences, all moments of our lives are loaded and should be treated as such, for they all hold within them the seeds for life and for death. It is our judgment that decides which.

And then, sometimes, we just get plain ol' lucky.

Chapter Four

It is now 5:00 Saturday morning. We have had five hours of labor! Time to call Jackie, our midwife, and let her know Baby Benedict is on its way. She is not happy to hear my voice.

Jackie is an excellent midwife. Unfortunately there is one thing she likes more than delivering babies and that's delivering blows. To say that Jackie is into martial arts is to put it mildly. She's a fanatic. Karate is to her what gossip is to Hollywood; she can't exist without it. She has been studying it for years, has her black belt, and practices with the commitment of a Mother Teresa. For some strange reason I found comfort in the fact that the woman who will be delivering our baby is capable of breaking boards, of destroying men twice her size with a single blow. After all, I tell myself, the study of martial arts takes discipline, patience, passion—all good qualities for a midwife. But there is a downside to this passion of hers. It takes precedence over all things in her life. *All things.*

Let me go back six months. Our midwife came highly recommended. She's young, healthy, attractive, intelligent. She's done hundreds of home births and shares our belief in a holistic lifestyle. No drugs, no sugar, no animal food, no chemicals. All natural. We speak the same language. The perfect person to deliver our baby. There is just one hitch. We can't, she informs us, have this baby on February 27. Toni and I laugh. What a quirky sense of humor she has. She isn't laughing. This is serious. We can have our baby on any day of the year except one . . . February 27! I ask the obvious question. She explains that February 27 is the date of a black-tie bash being held at the Bonnaventure Hotel in downtown Los Angeles. An extravaganza that will be attended by every major martial arts person in the world! Chuck Norris will be there, for crying out loud. She can't, simply *cannot,* miss this event! We laugh again. No problem. What are the odds of that happening? Besides, according to the experts, our due date is well before that. We assure her that come February 27 she will be boogeying with Chuck baby and we will be goo-goo-ing with our baby.

So it is with some trepidation that at 5:00 in the morning on the 27th of February, I inform her that Baby Benedict is on its way. The information is met with silence. Uh oh, I think I've just given her some bad news. She groans. Very, very bad news. For whom, I wonder? I feel like asking if she'd like to trade places. She tells us to time the contractions. I'm way ahead of her.

"They're three minutes apart!"

"Three minutes?"

"Three minutes."

"This can't be happening to me."

She tells us to keep timing the contractions. If there is a change, call her. Otherwise she'll come to our house around noon. I hear the urgency in her voice and know what she's thinking. Maybe the baby can be born before the banquet. If not, it will have to be born after the banquet. Because, as she firmly reminds me, "I told you, I cannot miss this banquet!" She can't mean this. Babies come when they come, they know nothing about Chuck Norris. They demand that life revolves around them. Push comes to birth, Jackie will give up her black-belt bash. Won't she? I'm beginning to get the Chuck Norris Blues. The butterflies in my stomach move over to make room for a brand new, tiny, little, itsy-bitsy sensation that I know only too well. Fear. I quickly deny it, push it aside. Not now. I assure Toni that we will be parents long before Jackie makes her sweeping entrance into Karate Heaven.

I know what it means to not want to miss a good party. The Saturday night before my Father's Sunday-morning demise there was a helluva beer party that I just had to go to. I'd been working all day stacking bales. I was thirsty. For beer, for my friends, for fun, and most important, though I didn't admit it, for relief from the pressures of having a Father who knew too much.

It was 1963, the summer before my freshman year at college. Cynthia, my high school sweetheart, and I were separated by 150 miles, as her parents had moved to Billings after our high school graduation. We hadn't seen one another all summer. She was in town. It would be our last weekend together before we swore eternal devotion and went off to separate institutions of higher learning. All of our friends would be there. All the hits of this pre-Beatle summer would be playing on the record player. Dancing, drinking, romancing, escaping . . . I couldn't wait.

I knew that the following day, Sunday, I had promised my Father that he and I would go fishing. I also knew that I had promised my Mother I would spend the day stacking more hay bales. Since my parent's divorce, my Mother was concerned that I make as much money as I could because my Father had "given all his away" and it was important I take every possible opportunity to make up for his failure to "hold up his end."

What my Father had in fact given away was more real than money. He gave away his reputation. His name. Gave away a private law practice that he had spent a lifetime building, and reflected the sum total of everything he had worked for in his professional life. He was known throughout the state of Montana as a lawyer of integrity and principle, of stubbornness and eccentricity. To know him was to love him. Or hate him. He had many enemies and many friends. Both passionate. His friends came from all walks of life, all economic strata. It didn't matter if you were an alcoholic sheepherder, an Indian (now Native American) ranch hand fresh off the reservation, or the governor of Montana. He treated everyone the same. If he was your lawyer, you knew he would defend you with honesty and passion. He'd been praised and vilified. He loved a good fight and was known as a friend of the powerless, the "little people." Held in contempt of court by the Supreme Court of Montana, he spent days in jail, all the while feasting on the pies and cakes sent to him by clients or the wives of clients he'd represented. No one who knew him was without an opinion or feeling about him. It would make for a strange and eclectic mix at his funeral later that summer . . . but I'm getting ahead of my story.

He gave away his money, his law practice . . . and he gave away his family. If it is possible to give away that which is no longer yours. The divorce, two years earlier, had taken care of that. With the divorce, the three children were forced to do the impossible . . . choose sides. I chose not to choose, and became a traitor to both camps. A boy without a family. Three meals a day, a warm bed and clean clothes, good grades and lots of friends—but no family. My high school graduation picture had something very wrong with it. But you had to look behind the eyes.

The complementary antagonisms between man and woman, husband and wife, that push them together and pull them apart have evaded comprehension by any and all experts. It has made psychiatrists rich, marriage counselors pull their hair, and divorce courts full to overflowing. But I knew none of this. I was eighteen years old, the fair-haired middle child of divorced parents who loved them both, and I thought I could work a miracle. Philosophically I was my Father's son, but alas, I had not cut the cord. That was yet to come.

But for now, the Saturday-night beer party with my high school sweetheart seemed the perfect way to hold off the reality of an overbooked Sunday, when I would have to be, *once again, all things to all people. Do what my Father wanted. Do what my Mother wanted. Doing what I wanted was a third option that long ago I learned to keep to myself. Or do covertly, as on this Saturday night, when what I wanted was for the world to go away. The world of parents and larger decisions regarding my life's direction. What I wanted was to pretend it wasn't happening. And so I did. I went to the party. Drank too much, danced too much, made innocent love to my sweetheart too much. And when the drinking and dancing and loving just had to end, as all things must, I despaired, and went home. Too much.*

"Poncho Musgrove called," said my Mother, who always waited up no matter how late I came home. "He'll pick you up at 8:00." I don't answer.

"You haven't forgotten you're stacking hay with him tomorrow," she said.

"No," I said. No matter how much fun the party, how much the romance, how hard the drinking . . . I hadn't forgotten. Anything. And then the big question, the question I knew was coming and had been asked of me since I could remember. . . .

"What are you going to tell your Dad?"

Silence. I said nothing but went to my room instead. And drowned.

How could she ask me the question she knew had no answer? For if there was one, why hadn't she given it to him? Years earlier? Given it to him on their wedding day? If not sooner? Given him the answer to all those irritating questions he kept asking? Kept asking by the simple fact that he kept breathing. His very existence a reminder that things were "wrong." Not the way they should be. Not the way he wanted them. Why didn't she give him what he needed to know? Needed to have? Needed. So that he would stop asking!

In the silence of the small upstairs bedroom we'd shared all our lives, I listened to my Brother's heavy, asthmatic breathing as he slept his tormented sleep in the few remaining hours allowed him before he would unload his rage, his terror, his heart.

I undressed in careful silence, as if by not waking my Brother this would all become a dream. Crawled under the covers with the dread that makes death a possible solution. I closed my eyes in dreadful anticipation, knowing that with the sun, my Father would arrive to ask his younger Son, once again, to do the impossible. To fulfill the promise. . . . To give up my Self and be all things to all people.

How could I have known what would happen? How could I not have known? Eighteen years of "experience" had prepared me for many variations on the theme. But not this one. Eighteen years that I could remember, if tortured into it, and in those eighteen years, everything had been said. By everyone. Endlessly. The family masquerade had become increasingly more difficult to maintain. Finally it became impossible. The mask came off. The pretense of a happy marriage, after twenty-five years, gave way to the reality of an acrid divorce and we all pretended to go our separate ways. My Father left to follow his dream and write his "book." To discover what it was he really wanted to do with his life before he was sidetracked by a successful law practice and an unsuccessful marriage.

I was two weeks away from playing in the Montana State East-West All-Star Football Game, then off to Whitman College in Walla Walla, Washington. My Brother, after all the years of college, the miserable years studying to be what he had no aptitude or inclination for, was finally going to become what he had always wanted to be. A carpenter. Why could my Father see only the lack of talent my Brother had for reading and writing and not the wealth of talent he had to build any and all things with his hands? Why couldn't my Father see the similarity between his own professional misery as an attorney and what would be my Brother's as the teacher he obediently went to college to become. Unlike my Father, my Brother still knew what he really wanted to do with his life. And though something was in his way, it wouldn't be for long.

That Sunday morning would change all our plans. My Father would go to Heaven (Hell, some would say). My Brother would replace his dream of carpentry with the nightmare of Vietnam. My Sister would run to the next-door neighbor, the next relationship, husband, and job. Run that she might escape the inescapable. And my Mother . . . my Mother would go silent. Something she knew very well how to do, knew very well was the loudest thing she had ever done. And all the pretenses would finally be once and forever given up and the truth of our family would be out. Known to all. Even us.

So I went to bed late, too late, with the taste of my sweetheart on my lips and the fear of morning in my soul. Fear. Fear of facing the wrath of my Father. The disappointment of my Mother. The truth of my Self. To fish or not to fish was the question. To be or not to be was the answer. I prayed I could, as I had for eighteen years, walk the tightrope. Stack the hay, catch the fish, and make everyone happy. Even if it drove me deeper into my own misery.

A stone on my upstairs bedroom window would be my wake-up call. An exploding big-game rifle would be the starting gun for the race to save my Self, even as it would mark the end for my Father, the family, and all that had gone before.

Chapter Five

I t is now nearly 2:00 Saturday afternoon. Toni and I have been through fourteen hours of labor. The contractions have been continuous, always three to five minutes apart, thirty to forty-five seconds in length. I have been cooking, cleaning, answering the telephone. Toni has been . . . contracting. The big question is always . . . how much dilation has taken place? This will tell us how close we are to having our baby. At 2:00 p.m., Jackie arrives in a flurry. She is not a happy person. She examines Toni. Only three centimeters dilated! I look at Jackie. Toni looks at Jackie. Jackie looks away.

"This is going to be a long labor."

Toni and I look at each other. "Going to be a long labor?" I mutter. Jackie pretends not to hear. She has her agenda.

"You've been in labor for fourteen hours and have only dilated three centimeters. I'm afraid this is just going to be a very slow-progressing labor. But then I told you that this would probably happen."

She did? I look to Toni. Toni smiles, nods yes to my questioning face. I reach out and wipe nonexistent sweat from her brow. Then I wipe the real stuff from my own. I must be very careful. I don't want Toni to pick up on any of my fears or anxieties. It is important to be positive. I begin to see for the first time that this journey is going to be very different for Toni than it is for me. How could I have missed that? "We" are not going to have a baby. Toni is going to have a baby. I am going to assist. Help. Watch.

I rationalize. Men are just not cut out for this. We were not meant to handle this kind of pressure! I am asking too much of myself. Sure Toni is doing all the work. But she is a woman, she has no choice! And anyway, she is designed for it, for the miracle of birth. It is, after all, in this age of dwindling sexual polarity, the last and only thing that separates us. Like all men, I am outside of it. Outside waiting, watching, and helpless.

Maybe this was all a mistake. I should be sitting in a bar with my friends, passing out cigars while I wait for the phone to ring. Do I actually have to be a part of the process? Wasn't it enough I planted the seed? Sure I believe in taking responsibility for one's life. Wrote a goddamned book about it. But taking responsibility for the lives of others? For Toni and the young soul inside her waiting for its moment to be born into this world? This is something I hadn't considered. I understand that love is putting the lives of others, those you love, ahead of yours. That you will give everything you have, everything you are, even your very life, for them, to them. I understand that. But I have never actually done it.

So now, by taking responsibility for the birth of this child, born of the woman I love, I have unknowingly trapped myself in a situation where the depth of my love will be tested. Horrors! I am about to learn the truth. My love has made me responsible. Not the midwife or the doctors, but me . . . I am responsible. I could have, like most husbands, simply handed my wife over to a hospital. Waited for them to hand her and the child back. But by doing so, am I not saying, "I don't love you"? Not enough to take responsibility for your life, for your death. I draw the line there; let me fill out the forms and hand you over to others. I will be responsible for holding *them* responsible. This is, after all, America—land of the free, home of the lawyer. Should anything go wrong, I'll hire the best damn lawyer money can buy. Then I'll hold *him* responsible for holding the doctor responsible. From the doctor to the lawyer. From the frying pan to the fire.

It doesn't matter, just get me off the hook! I start to sing to myself . . .

> Just let me, get me, off the hook,
> Off the hook of love.

The hook of love. Did my Father give his life so that I might have mine? Don't all fathers? All parents? In one way or another? Over a lifetime? Or in an instant? By changing a diaper? Or biting a bullet? Wasn't that what my Father's eyes said as they looked into mine in that last moment when nothing existed? Nothing. Not the morning sun; not the joy of fishing or the agony of not fishing; not the dilemma of fathers and sons, and mothers and sons, or the infinite riddle of human failure. When all that existed was a split second that lasted an eternity, that lasts to this day. A split second that would be simultaneously the last time I saw him and the first time I'd ever really seen him! And what I saw in his eyes, as he let me off the hook of love, I have never seen since. But then I've never since looked into the eyes of a dying man. Never seen eyes that say life and death no longer matter. No longer are different. No longer exist. And in that endless infinitesimal speck of time, I knew it was over.

As I unraveled, pounded the side of the garage with the pent-up rage and frustration of eighteen years, and heard him through my sobbing anger as he broke and entered what he had had the key to for twenty-five years, hunting for what he had lost in another home in another time in his own childhood, I sensed, beyond it all, that this is where it would all begin for me and that I was now, and forevermore, off the hook of my love for him.

That he so loved his middle begotten son . . . that when all his examples failed, when all the words had failed, the attempts at reconciliation, the struggle to pretend to a happiness that didn't exist; that when all else had failed, and finally realizing he had failed himself, he knew only his death would succeed.

How he knew (if he knew) the .243 Savage was loaded and waiting while my Mother slept, loaded and waiting lo these twenty-five years, I don't know. Nor does it matter. Because he would get his; it was only a matter of time and a question of caliber. Because it was his family, and my Father had a lifetime to know where danger lurked. Who *slept in what bed. Where the guns were kept. And what son was his Mother's boy. And he would not be denied, he would get his!*

All this I could feel as I drank and loved that long-ago Saturday night of teenage revelry, desperately trying to keep the sun from rising. But Sunday came.

And now, twenty-five years later, waiting for my first child to be born, it comes once again. And with it, all the forgotten memories I pretend to have laid to rest. All the fervent attempts to rid me of my Father's ghost.

Sunday. Sun Day.
Father and Son Day.
Day of life. Day of death.
Day of birth. Day of . . . rest?

Not likely. Jackie explains why this is going to be a long labor. I've heard it all before. She tells us to remain calm, be patient, and remember, "I'm only a telephone call away." I see her spirits lift as she realizes she is going to meet Chuck Norris after all. For the first time, I notice the beeper strapped to her belt.

"Are you sure?" I ask, not quite ready to lose her to Chuckie baby and the charisma of his black belt.

"Quite sure," she says.

Is she really this confident or is it merely the thought of Chuck that makes her seem like she is? I know that it is up to me to make the final decision. The ball has bounced into my side of the court. Do I let her go or do I insist that she remain here with us? My understanding of the situation from what I've read, and my judgment of her abilities make me believe that it *is* going to be a long labor. But how much more can Toni handle? How long before she starts to get tired, to weaken?

"Okay. We'll call if the contractions become one minute apart."

I have done my homework. I am ready to face the truth. Because the bottom line, of course, is that, if necessary, I can deliver the baby. Without this belief, the decision to have a baby at home would be foolish. That is, after all, the whole point.

Jackie assures me that the baby will not be born until early Sunday morning. My mind swerves.

Sunday. Sun Day. Father and Son Day. . . .

Never mind. Sunday . . . I calculate . . . that's twelve hours away. My God! That would mean twenty-eight hours of labor! Up till now, Toni has been full of vigor and humor and a positive attitude. But everyone has his limits. When will Toni reach hers? And what about me? We all know women are stronger than men, more enduring. I shouldn't have spent all day Friday trying to finish the stupid screenplay. Where will I get the energy for this baby? Oh, baby! Time to call Laurie.

Jackie agrees. Laurie is a true veteran when it comes to having babies. She's had four, all of them in the delivery room she calls home. She's also our next-door neighbor and a close friend of Toni. We have asked her to attend the birth to assist Jackie and me. There are so many little things that need to be done during a birth that you can always use another set of hands. Especially if they've already been there.

We call Laurie. No answer. Check the number. Try again. Still no answer. Impossible. Laurie and her husband are always home. They have four children, for crying out loud. There has to be somebody at home. Besides, Laurie knows the baby is due any day now. Then Toni remembers that Laurie had asked if we thought the baby was coming this weekend. Toni told her that Jackie didn't think the baby would be born until the first week of March. (Certainly not *this* weekend; Chuck baby is in town.) We keep calling. Where could Laurie and her entire family have gone? We call mutual friends. Bad news. Don and Laurie have gone to Disneyland with the kids. For the entire weekend! If it isn't Chuck Norris, it's Mickey Mouse!

Now what? "Not to worry," says Jackie. As soon as she gets home she will call a professional birth attendant she sometimes uses and send her in our direction.

"Why not call now?" I ask.

"I don't have the number with me," she says and assures us the attendant will show up around 6:00 p.m. Toni and I will have to go it alone for only a couple more hours.

So that's the plan. Jackie will go to her black-belt adventure at the Bonnaventure, while Toni and I remain behind in our misadventure and wait for the attendant. Jackie assures us once again (my skepticism must be showing) that she will be able to get from her banquet at the hotel to our house in the boondocks in less than an hour.

Just one last thing. . . . she doesn't have a dress that is really right for a black-tie affair; could she borrow Toni's cute little Azzedine Alaïa that she had seen during one of her prenatal visits to our home? I grit my teeth. Martial arts and gall go hand in hand. Toni seems unfazed. She goes to get the gown between contractions. Jackie is thrilled. It's so sexy, the perfect outfit for her martial arts shindig. She's beside herself. She should be; I know how much the damn dress cost.

Jackie carries Toni's dress, caressing it with her eyes as I walk her to her car. It is now about 4:00 p.m. Not much time for her to get ready. She gives me the number for her beeper and tells me not to worry; she'll be back in plenty of time. She figures she can drive from the hotel to our home, which is fifty miles away in the high desert mountains northeast of Los Angeles, in about forty-five minutes. I look at her little Japanese import. It might have been built since the war, but looks as if it's been through it. She follows my look. "Well, maybe an hour," she concedes, "but that will be plenty of time."

Time? It is now 4:00 in the afternoon! Sixteen hours of labor. I thought we would have had our baby by now. Instead our midwife is en route for a rendezvous with Chuck baby while I'm left with the number of the beeper strapped to her black-belted Azzedine Alaïa, which will soon, if she has her way, be in the muscular arms of Chuck Norris.

As she gets into her vintage import, I notice the left front tire is bald. Just what I need to see. I flash on bald tires sliding on rain-drenched freeways, on flat tires and stranded midwives. A stormy, rainy weekend may create romantic ambience, but it also stirs the imagination. Am I ready to deliver this baby? Am I in over my head? (When haven't I been?) Am I ready for the truth? My Father's voice . . .

It's always the unloaded gun!

These and other thoughts permeate my brain as Jackie grinds gears and chugs down our gravel driveway, my wife's gown flapping in the seat beside her. The Karate Party Kid. I lift my face into the falling rain, fill my lungs with cool air, and my mind drifts back to my first brush with passage into poppadom.

Chapter Six

I thought "Immaculate Conceptions" were ancient history. The Bible told me so. Cynthia Louise Sanders, my high school sweetheart and the youngest daughter of Zack Sanders, would tell me different. Never date a Catholic girl if you don't believe in miracles.

Zack Sanders had a ranch near U.S. Highway 12 about thirty miles east of White Sulphur Springs. Keep driving east and you come to Billings. It would be nearly a decade before I'd learn that if you drove even further into the rising sun you'd come to a place called New York, which was to the world what Billings was to Montana. But that was yet to be. New York was not part of my dream but vaguely a place where dudes came from and tall buildings grew.

Owning a ranch in Meagher County, of which White Sulphur Springs was the county seat, was about as unusual as being on a diet if you live in America. What made Zack Sanders' ranch unique was that back in the 1930s, it had been a dude ranch. And what made it special as a dude ranch were the herds of buffalo and elk that roamed the place. The dudes came by train from exotic places like Los Angeles, New York, and Chicago. Local cowboys would ride the elk and buffalo as they slid some fifty or sixty feet down a chute into a lake. This caused quite a splash with the ladies and gents from Park Avenue, Lake Shore Drive, and Wilshire Boulevard. Rope tricks, roundups, fishing, hunting, and "roughing it" were also available for the dudes and dudettes, but it was the buffalo-elk slide that really put the place on the map. (The dude ranches of yesteryear have been replaced with the "second home" ranches and ranchettes of the middle and upper classes, who continue to want their croissants and pancakes, too.)

During my high school years (1959–1963), the Sanders' ranch had long since ceased to be a playground for city slickers. It was just another cattle ranch in a land of cattle ranches. And although they had long since retired from show business, the buffalo and elk still considered the ranch their home on the range. Their life was pretty good, except for the annual buffalo-elk barbecue, for which several of them would be asked to appear.

The ranch was a great place to get a buffalo burger. It was also the place of choice for our summer weekend parties. A case of Great Falls Select beer, a record player, a stack of 45s, and we would drink, dance, and romance for free in the same old log inn where decades earlier dudes had paid top dollar to do the same. It would be years before

I realized how truly unique and romantic it was as my classmates and I danced in the moonlit, crystal-clear air, drunk with the smell of pine and the thrill of youth. We rocked to Elvis while the buffalo roamed and the deer and the antelope played. Elvis never had it so good. Neither did we.

Cynthia Sanders and I started going steady during our sophomore year. She was my first real girlfriend. She wore my class ring. We went out exclusively with each other. We were as "meant for each other" as two kids could be in a town where the population was 1,000; the high school enrollment, 125; the number of kids in your class, 30; and the number of girls your age, 12. Cynthia was one of the 12 and the pick of the litter. She had it all. Beauty, brains . . . and brawn! Five foot nine, 135 pounds, broad shoulders, slim hips . . . this girl also packed one helluva punch! She could out arm-wrestle all but the strongest members of our football team. Not the kind of girl from whom one could easily wrestle virginity. Not that I didn't try. Not that she didn't want me to try.

Back in those days only "bad girls" went "all the way." But if you were in love, had his ring on your finger, his tongue in your mouth, and his hand on your breast, well . . . the line between good and bad could become very, very blurred. We lived in a blurred state of sexual apprehension. And dread. If it was bad, how come it felt so good? I was as afraid of the situation as Cynthia was, but it would have been unmanly, a break of the Montana male code of behavior, to express such fears. So I persisted and she resisted as we struggled time and again to appease the gods of sexual satiation without losing a clear conscience and an intact hymen. Not an easy trick.

Because our relationship had everything but sex, eventually the inevitable happened and it became about nothing except sex. Less became more. Much more. With each year our "problem" became greater. A simple kiss goodnight would immediately find our teenage bodies panting, screaming for more. Holding hands became sexual foreplay. Saying no at sixteen, when you've first "fallen in love," is one thing; at eighteen, after two years of "being in love," it becomes something entirely different. And don't forget (because we never did) that Cynthia was Catholic. Saying no, no matter how naked and wanting she was on the leather backseat of a 1955 Chrysler New Yorker, was made possible because saying yes meant eternal damnation. To say nothing of the wrath of Zack Sanders, her dominating father, should he ever find out that his youngest daughter, the apple of his eye and virginal gift to the world, had given herself, her body, not in the sanctity of a marriage bed, but in the steamy backseat of a '55 Chrysler. Which would be worse? The wrath of God or the wrath of Zack? As much as we both wanted the riddle of our sexual dilemma answered, neither one of us wanted to find out the answer to "that" question.

Somehow, by the grace of God, the wrath of Zack, and with much wear and tear on the Chrysler's backseat, we managed to keep our sexual graduation on the back burner as we graduated from high school to go our separate ways into the halls of higher learning. Cynthia to Montana State in Bozeman; I to Whitman College in Walla Walla.

Distance and time helped cool the fire of our perpetual

passion. We dated other people. I discovered girls from other religions. Girls that, lo and behold, dove with glee into the joys of fulfilling their sexual selves. This was, after all, the 1960s, the dawning of female liberation. Good girls and bad girls were no longer defined by whether or not they went all the way. They all went wherever they wanted, whenever they wanted, and were happy to take you along. Their sexual destinies were no longer in the double-standard hands of a hypocritical society created by double-dealing men. Let men eat Wheaties; for women, the breakfast of champions was the Pill. What a way to start the day. Have orgasms, not babies! Sex was in. Virginity was out. Very, very out. Girls everywhere were desperate to make up for all their mothers' lost orgasms, for all the no's, which, they knew with the first purchase of an IUD, had really meant yes all along! Orgasms were no longer singular and clitoral but multiple and vaginal. The dynamics had indeed changed.

Everything I'd learned with Cynthia in our backseat sex-education class was turned upside down. I wondered how she was handling it? What was she having for breakfast? Was Poppa Zack still God? If you are once a Catholic, are you always a Catholic? With the summer of '65, I would soon have the answer to these and other, more intimate, questions.

The summer of the Immaculate Conception. I was working for the United States Forest Service, making money to support my college education and the pursuit of my new-found interest in acting. Cynthia was home from college and living in Billings, where her family had moved after our graduation from high school two years earlier. There's a phone call. She's happy to hear my voice. I am more than happy to hear hers. We begin again. Every other weekend or so I drive my Mother's new car to Billings to see her. The '55 Chrysler has become a '64 Chrysler 300. It is very fast and has a very small backseat. Cynthia and I are both testing the waters. (But not the backseat.) Is anything left from our high school romance? The times have changed. We have changed. Is it possible to pick up the pieces? Start over?

Cynthia's parents had bought a beautiful, sprawling home in the "nice" part of Billings. It had more luxuries than I had ever seen. Air conditioning, an electric garage door, a swimming pool, an automatic ice maker! It even had a circular drive! Paved!

It is early August. Her parents are away. Cynthia has a small party. I drive down for it. A chance to meet some of her new friends from college. There is music, laughter, dancing, and lots of sharing of college experiences and touching and kissing and finally Cynthia and I are alone. The circular drive is empty. (Except for the Chrysler 300 with the small backseat.) The beer is gone. The lights are low. The music is Johnny Mathis. The ice maker is out of ice . . . things are heating up. And the inevitable happens.

The sexual revolution may have started, but it started without Cynthia, and I have the answer to one of my questions . . . once a Catholic, always a Catholic.

Her no's drift softly beneath Johnny Mathis's soaring rendition of "Misty." No's dripping with yes. With yes, yes, yes. Moving, directing my hands over her body as she moans for me to stop. To stop a little faster. Pull it out a little deeper.

What was I to do? I wasn't Catholic, but years of taking no for an answer had me very well trained. No had always meant no. Not right away perhaps, but finally, when push came to enter, it always, always meant stop. And I always listened. And obeyed. I wanted to do what she wanted to do. Did she still know what she wanted?

Eyes closed. Some part of her saying one thing, while another part of her says . . . another. Says yes. I am confused. And fearful. Of the consequences. Of the wrath of Zack. Fearful that I will discover, afterward, that I don't really love her. And I do know that if I don't, then no must always be the answer. No matter who says it. Nonetheless. . . .

Four years of foreplay have led us to this moment in this living room on this couch on this hot Montana summer night as we wrestle with our coital karma. Johnny isn't helping things, as his sensual tenor croons to musical climax. The couch on which we writhe is wet with moisture from orifices we never knew existed. Her no's, now a continual primitive chant, have become her sexual mantra. She waits, eyes closed, for me to seize the moment and take her, take us, into our future. I hesitate. And I hesitate. And the hesitation becomes the moment. And as I finally decide, give in to the years of wanting, throw caution to the wind and Johnny Mathis, begin to enter into the future and let go of the past . . . I come. I come and the moment goes and the eyelids open and the clothes are back on . . . and our future just passed.

Or so I thought. I should have known, given the guilt that engulfed Cynthia as we hugged and kissed good-bye, that this wasn't the end of it. I should have known, as I drove down the circular drive, that this too would come full circle.

I thought my supremely premature ejaculation had solv-

ed all our problems. Gotten us out of the dilemma of to do or not to do. To have and not to have. But I was wrong.

I decided on my drive back to White Sulphur Springs in the early hours of the morning that the evening of coitus interruptus was to be my last visit to Billings and the sexual turmoil that lived there. We loved each other too much to say no, too little to say yes. I was determined to tell her this. I never found the words.

The summer waned. The phone rang.

"I'm pregnant."

"What?"

"I'm pregnant."

"What?" I hear a shotgun ringing in my ear.

"I've had tests and I'm pregnant."

"Tests?" I switch the phone to my good ear.

"I'm pregnant." I switch back.

"Cynthia, it's impossible. I didn't . . . we didn't . . . it's impossible."

"What are we going to do?"

I want to ask her what she eats for breakfast. But I know I should have asked long before this. Before the couch when the ice ran out and things heated up and Johnny Mathis grew misty.

It was an Immaculate Conception as far as I was concerned and there hadn't been one of those in years. But what did I know? I was twenty years old, could count my sexual experiences on two fingers, and was by no means an expert in these matters. My limited understanding of the process of impregnation was that the penis had to enter the vagina in order for the sperm to have a chance to reach the egg. I *tried to share my limited understanding of this process with Cynthia.*

Won't you listen to me, honey?
'Cuz I'm sure I've got this right.
And it could keep us both
From many sleepless nights.

Without the penis in vagina
There's no sperm in the egg,
There's no baby come between us,
Won't you listen, please? I beg.

She would have none of it. Obviously I didn't know what I was rhyming about. I began to doubt myself. How close do sperm have to get to be within striking distance? In the same room? On the same couch? Can sperm be absorbed through the skin? Passive procreation! But she's Catholic, not Jewish, and anything but passive. But she is pregnant. So she says. Her period has been days, then weeks, late. Her panic turns into hysteria. I can hear it over the phone. She went for tests. The rabbit died. I feel I am about to.

By some impossible means, Cynthia was pregnant. Or so the doctor said. She told her mother. She told the pastor of her church. She was telling me. God, I assumed, already knew. There was only one person who had yet to know. Oh, Zack!

After work, over a period of several weeks, I would grab a quick shower, jump in my Mother's car, and drive the 156 miles to Billings, where Cynthia and I would discuss, endlessly, our options. There weren't that many. She wanted to get married. I did not. It took many hours of talk to finally say it, many more to try to explain. Having buried my Father only two years previous, I was not capable of imagining myself becoming one. My problems were many and deep. My attempt to deal with them was only just beginning. Further, I dreamed of seeing what lay at the end of U.S. Highway 12, of becoming an actor, of finding out who I was. I did not dream of becoming a husband, a father. Yet it seemed, in the eyes of the Church, through the miracle of an Immaculate Conception, I had.

This Immaculate Conception was getting very messy. It was an impossible situation. I was heartsick. She was heart-broken. Endless hours of discussion led to the tearful decision that she would have the child. (Abortion was never considered. It was illegal in the eyes of the law, forbidden in the eyes of the Church, and much as I was terrified of marriage and fatherhood, I didn't like the idea myself.) I would share my responsibility in absentia: contribute financially, be the father of record, give the child my name if Cynthia wanted it. (She didn't.) Visit her and the child as long as and whenever it was possible. Absentee fatherhood. I was so naive. So stupid. So scared.

With the dread of one on the way to his own hanging I drove to Billings, for the last time, to be with Cynthia when we told the one person who didn't know that his daughter was pregnant and that I was the culprit, the boy who had wrecked her life, besmirched the family name. I was still, in the face of all the hysteria and scientific proof, claiming she couldn't be pregnant. I might as well have been claiming the Earth was flat. I was beating a very dead rabbit.

Zack Sanders' reaction to the unwanted good news that his angelic daughter was with child was not as bad as I had anticipated. He had no intention of maiming or torturing me. He just wanted to kill me. Wanted me gone. From his daughter's life, from the face of the Earth. Cynthia and her mother came to my rescue, came between him and his desire to drown me in their beautiful swimming pool.

Cynthia walked me to my car while her father raged in the backyard. I hated myself for what I had done as much as for what I hadn't done. As we hugged (but didn't kiss) good-bye, I was struck by the sensation that the pain of this experience was the most intimate thing Cynthia and I had ever shared. Much more profound than any tussle we had had on any couch or backseat. I was overwhelmed with love for her, for us. I wanted to tell her. Instead, I climbed into my car and drove down the paved circular driveway, knowing that the circle, and so much, much more, had been broken. Forever.

But that was not the end of the story, and I am not the absentee father of a child born out of the passion and turmoil of a hot summer night in Montana twenty-eight years ago.

A month later I am back in Walla Walla for the start of my junior year. I have just returned from my last class of the afternoon. The phone rings at the fraternity house where I live. It's Cynthia. I set down my books. I am glad she has called. The sound of her voice is wonderful. This surprises me and I wonder if maybe there is another solution other than absentee fatherhood.

"Dirk?"

"Cynthia . . ."

"I'm not pregnant." I switch ears.

"I've started my period," she says matter-of-factly.

I look for a place to sit down.

The world is flat. The rabbit is alive. It was all a dream . . . passive procreation, premature ejaculation, fatherly abnegation . . . all of it. What isn't a dream and what we both know is that our relationship has been destroyed. All the years growing up together, all the moments that we shared as we went steady and lived the excitement of our youth and that will never come again or be shared with others as completely as they had been with each other . . . all that is gone. No class reunions. No laughter on mutual reflection of what we once were. Separately and together. Whole chapters of our lives are lost and gone forever.

"I'm sorry, Dirk."

"I'm sorry, too."

There is nothing else to say. So we say it. We hang up on each other. Never again to be hung up on each other.

Hysterical pregnancy! That's what the doctors called it. Cynthia had convinced herself so completely that she was pregnant that she changed the chemistry of her blood. Maybe it was wishful thinking? I don't know. I do know that with that kind of mental power she will never have to worry about cancer. Hysterical pregnancy. Mind over matter. I still find it hard to believe. Maybe you have to be Catholic? Maybe . . . wait a minute . . . maybe it was all Johnny Mathis's fault? Not the Church, not the hysteria of a girl convinced that premarital sex was eternal damnation, not the inexperienced, naive flounderings of a tormented Montana boy, but Johnny Mathis and the sexual resonance of his romantic croon? I don't know, maybe not. I do know this: I have never since listened to Johnny Mathis, and I have yet to have another hysterical pregnancy in my life. So who knows?

Everything goes in circles. Not only driveways but life. Four years later, in 1969, during the Labor Day Weekend Rodeo in White Sulphur Springs, Cynthia and I bump into each other. Sheer coincidence as neither of us has been around much in the past years. I'm on my way to my first professional acting gig in Seattle, and she's engaged to be married in a couple of months.

It's 2:00 a.m. in the Melody Lane Bar. We sit barstool to barstool, heart to heart, and attempt to forgive ourselves our human frailty over whiskey and beer. We're both laughing through tears, on the verge of soulful reconciliation, when suddenly I am yanked backward off my barstool and flat onto my back amongst the spilled beer and cigarette butts. My attacker is a woman gone mad, pummeling me as she screams, DYou've drug our family through enough dirt, you sonofabitch! You stay away from my sister."

Samantha "Sam" Sanders, Cynthia's sister and possessed of the same broad shoulders, had entered the bar and taken exception to our cozy confab. She is beating the hell out of me (and religion in? For she, too, is Catholic) when her boyfriend Matt, a robust logger, drags her off me and out the door, kicking and screaming all the way. I guess hysteria runs in the family.

Needless to say, the moment had been ruined. Cynthia got married. I became a professional actor. We have yet to finish our barstool commiseration. But I do know this: You were right, Cynthia; I should have said yes. And you were wrong; you should have said no. No to everything that wasn't what you wanted, so that you could have had what you did want, and how and when you wanted it. And from our beginning to our end, I don't regret any of it.

This was my first brush with fatherhood. There would be others. Each serving to deepen my fear of it and my resolve to avoid it. For I knew that in becoming a father I would be forced to deal with the Ghost of Father Past.

Chapter Seven

With Jackie's departure for her black-tie shindig, Toni and I are once again alone. Our only company is the sound of the wind and the rain as it beats against the house. Four o'clock has come and gone, then five o'clock. Toni's contractions are three to five minutes apart and growing in intensity. She takes a hot bath to help her dilate. I talk to her, massage her lower back to ease the pain. I cook more food, do what I can to keep her comfortable. Comfortable? Hardly. But at least reassured. I am beginning to unravel a bit. Toni is still so positive and chipper, I feel guilty for my inner worries and doubts. "Everything is going to be fine," I keep telling myself. Toni asks me what I'm mumbling about. I do it silently. It becomes my mantra. Interrupted only by the phone, which seems to ring constantly.

The phone! I've always hated the phone and the easy

access it gives people into the private rhythms of your life. It makes everything more difficult, as it rings always when you least want it to. During a home birth, only God should have your number.

Ordinarily I would simply not answer, but the word is out. Everyone who has tried to talk us out of a home birth is calling to see how things are going. How things are going? Well, let's see, we've been in labor for eighteen hours, there is no midwife with us, we are fifty miles from town, and our birth attendant is in Disneyland. "Things" are going awry, that's how they're going! But I can't tell them that. It would trigger a deluge of unwanted advice. So I do what one always does in show business . . . tell them what they want to hear. In other words, lie like hell. It's easier, simpler, and faster. I lie about the length of time we have been in labor. Lie about the severity of the contractions. Lie about the whereabouts of our midwife. Lie about my state of mind. I even lie when asked if I'm lying. Some of my friends know me too well.

Again the phone rings. It's Jackie. Good news? No such luck. She can't find her beeper. Did she leave it at our house? What does that matter? I ask her. If it's here and you're there it's no good to anybody! But she's frantic to find her beeper. It's expensive! Without her beeper she's lost. Would I please look?

I want to scream, "To hell with the beeper! My wife's in the next room trying to have a baby while you're fifty miles away wearing her Azzadine Alaïa at a karate banquet with Chuck Norris asking me to find your beeper. Forget the goddamned beeper and get your martial-arts ass back here!"

I go look for the beeper. Toni goes into a contraction. I

hold her hand, talk to her. She resurfaces. Back to my beeper search. Nowhere to be found. I tell Jackie. She is frantic. For the first time since I've known this woman I hear something other than total calm and control in her voice. Those beepers must be real expensive.

Throughout all this controlled chaos Toni remains unbelievably calm and full of good humor. Her endurance is very real and definite. Inspiring. I wish more than ever that my Father could have met her. Maybe he will. Spiritually. What would he do in this situation? Where was he when I was born? How did he feel? What was he thinking? I am full of questions. What have I gotten us into? I begin to question my judgment, my entire philosophy of life. Is it mine or do I pretend to it in memory (fear?) of my Father? Kamikaze cowboy turns into yuppie putty. I resist crumbling. I am responsible here. Toni has trusted me, my judgment, and my belief in self and self-reliance.

Back to the missing beeper.

"Jackie, I can't find it. It isn't here. Now how in the hell am I going to call if I need you before your (goddamned) banquet is over?"

"Not to worry," she says. The calm is back in her voice. I can't help but feel relieved to hear it. She gives me the number of the hotel. She will inform them that she is waiting for a call and they should page her immediately. I hope she's not in the arms of Chuck when I call. Okay. Okay. I guess that'll have to do. Again she tells me not to worry. She assures me she will be at our place no later than 2:00 a.m. and she is certain Toni will not be going into transition before that time. Meanwhile she has called the professional birthing attendant, who should be arriving at our place within the hour. "This is going to be a" . . . I know, I know. I close my eyes, massage my forehead . . . "very long labor." As if it hasn't been already. I hang up the phone. I hope the birthing attendant arrives soon. I could use an extra set of hands.

Time passes and 6:00 p.m. arrives. Our professional birth attendant doesn't. When 6:00 p.m. becomes 7:00 p.m., I become fidgety. At 7:30 the phone rings. I get ready to lie. Who is this? Good news. Our birth attendant is on the other end of the line. But wait, what is this? She isn't just around the corner, as I had hoped, nor is she on her way. She's at a party. A birthday party. For her grandmother! Blithely, she explains she can't make it till around 9:00 p.m. Will that be all right? No, it won't be all right!

"There's only one birthday party I'm interested in and it isn't your grandma's!" Doesn't faze her. Everyone's going to parties. If it isn't Chuck Norris, it's Grandma. I'm trying to have a baby! Only the guest list keeps changing on me.

"Sure, go to your grandma's birthday," I say as I slam the phone down. What the hell is going on here? I rush back to comfort Toni.

The contractions get stronger, the back pain worse. To ease the pain, I administer hot packs to Toni's lower back. Give her a hot bath. Get her a change of clothes. It is crucial she keeps her strength. She must eat and drink. I cook food. I wash dishes. The phone rings. Fine, fine, fine, everything's fine. I lie about how normal everything is. Back to Toni. More contractions. Always more contractions, now almost a minute in length and getting stronger. Still three to five minutes apart. I monitor the baby's heartbeat. Strong, steady, and fast . . . about 140 to 160 beats a minute. Beautiful. The baby is strong.

Doesn't get it from me. I'm dead on my feet. Can't let it show. Strength . . . where will I get it? Toni is strong, amazing. Where does she get it? Proves what I've always suspected, women are stronger than men. She comforts *me* between her back-breaking contractions. Pain is never mentioned. It becomes a word without meaning, a nonword. Pain only exists when there is pleasure against which to compare it. There is no pleasure here, only the need to endure. And we endure alone.

Through the rain and wind I hear a doorbell. I look at the clock. It is 8:30 p.m. Like a prizefighter answering the fifteenth round, I shuffle to the door downstairs while Toni rests up for the next onslaught.

The professional has arrived! I had forgotten she was coming. Just in time. Grandma's party is over. Thank God. I am exhausted. The endless running, cooking, and worrying while I question every facet of my life's philosophy have taken their toll.

"You're here!" I state the obvious, remembering that my face has become an open book and the look on my face must tell her how relieved I am. Evidently not.

"Can I have something to drink?" she asks by way of greeting.

I'm flabbergasted. Saying no takes more energy than getting the tea. As she sips her tea, I run to attend to Toni. The professional ambles up the stairs, comes sipping into the bedroom, meets Toni and asks if maybe she might also have something to eat. Didn't Grandma have any refreshments at her party? But what the hell, I plan on working her to death; better make sure she is fed and watered. And I *am* so relieved she is here. After nearly twenty-four hours of waiting on Toni alone, I'm just happy to have someone, anyone, to keep us company. I fix her a bite to eat. (Perhaps I missed my true calling in life. Make a helluva short-order cook.) The professional has been fed; she has been quenched; I am dead on my feet. It is time for her to go to work.

Toni is still in good humor. Strong, steady . . . but for how long? I tell her I am going to lie down for a bit. She assures me she will be fine. I'm too tired to feel guilty. I trundle off to the couch in my office. I plan to sleep five or six hours while the professional stays with Toni. It is 9:30 p.m. I fall immediately into a sleep just this side of death. The couch becomes my coffin.

The coffin opens. I see my Father's face. It is 1963. I am eighteen years old and alone in the parlor of the Twichell Funeral Home. Well, not quite alone, if you believe in ghosts. Which I very soon will. It is the day before my father is to be "laid to rest."

Is being dead restful? The ultimate vacation? Or does it depend on how we lived? Do we have to earn our rest in the ever after, just as we earn our keep in the here and now?

It is the first time I have seen my father since I watched him, his shoes protruding from beneath a sheet, being carried out the front door of our family home. His eyes are closed. I am struck with the realization, not that he is dead (that will take years), but that he is so calm. It unnerves me. I've never seen him like this. Never seen him sleep. Or take a nap. Or in any kind of repose. I am overwhelmed with his loss of vitality. How full of everything he was. Including life. To see him so calm is stranger than death. Shakespeare wrote a play based on my relationship with my Father. (How did he know?) Twenty-five years later, in New York City, I will realize on stage my kinship with the character of Hamlet and understand only too well this, among other things:

> I knew him, Horatio——a fellow of infinite jest, of most excellent fancy. He hath borne me on his back a thousand times, and now, how abhorred in my imagination it is! My gorge rises at it. Here hung those lips that I have kissed I know not how oft. Where be your gibes now? Your gambols? Your songs? Your flashes of merriment that were wont to set the table on a roar?

Did my Father ever rest? Really rest? Maybe if he'd just taken a good nap on that Sunday, any Sunday, all this could have been avoided. And I wouldn't be in this awful, awkward position. Trying to say good-bye to my coffin-clad Father. The man who bounced me on his knee, taught me how to fish, how to play the piano, how to say no. Taught me how to think! How to live. And how to die? My mind races. It will race for years to come. How can I say good-bye when I refuse to accept that he is gone? My eyes are dry. They will be dry for years to come.

But for the lack of what we call life, he looks the same. I touch his face. Most of us can't feel life when it is with us. It is much easier to feel when it is gone. Never touch a dead person. It is touching the end. It makes you feel extremely fragile and very, very mortal. More mortal than I, at eighteen and consumed with rage, guilt, and fear, am prepared to be. My denial goes deep. Into my very bloodstream. Into the molecular structure of my being. Death escapes me, as life has escaped my Father. I notice instead his stubble. Remember hearing (reading) that our hair continues to grow after we are . . . wherever my Father is now. How strange. That hair should outlive the heart. (There may have been a deeper wisdom to the Native American art of scalping than met the white man's eye.) There are no words for what I am feeling because I am not feeling. Not this decade. My Dad needs a shave. I tell him so. Big problems. Small talk.

"I'm sorry, Dad. I was wrong. We should have gone fishing. Next time. (Next time?) I'll make this up to you. You'll see. I'll show everybody. You were right. All along. About everything. You were right."

Right and wrong. Good and bad. True and false. Life and death. All color, nuance, compromise drain from my life. Never touch a dead person. The world is black and white. I am resolute. My mind, emotions, psyche grow rigid. I become as stiff as my Father is . . . was? Future friends, lovers, teachers will wonder where all this black and white, all this ruthless, unyielding, adamant, intractable, bullheaded, pigheaded, hardheaded, perverse asceticism comes from. It comes from the grave. It comes with the territory. It goes . . . wherever I go.

Chapter Eight

T aylor and Rose Gordon were the only black people I ever saw or knew until I would finally follow
U.S. Highway 12 to its eastern end and discover
the melting pot of New York and the ethnicity that
stewed in it. Taylor had worked for the Ringling Brothers
Circus and when John Ringling built a summer home in
White Sulphur Springs in the 1930s, Taylor came with him
as his chauffeur. When Taylor retired, he came back to White
Sulphur Springs. Rose was his sister, and they lived together
in a little house just off Main Street.

Taylor had a magnificent baritone voice. When Mr.
Ringling became aware of this, he sent him to New York for
vocal training, and Taylor stopped driving for the rich and
began singing for them. He had a long career as an opera
singer. He sang in Carnegie Hall and toured throughout

Europe. The fascinating story of his life was told in his autobiography, "Born to Be." My Father often used him as an example of the infinite power of the human spirit to realize its dreams. That nothing was impossible if one believed. That one was limited only by the size of one's dream and the depth of one's commitment. How significant it would be for me to realize in later years that my Father had more in common with Taylor Gordon, a black man from the Deep South, isolated in this small ranching community in central Montana, than he did with the white lawyers, ranchers, and miners. He and Taylor Gordon were kindred spirits.

In the desperate days after my Dad's demise, I demanded that Taylor Gordon sing at the funeral. It wasn't a popular demand because, while a friend of my Father's, he was not close to the family. Nor was I. The familial rift that had been growing for as long as I could remember erupted into a full-blown schism with the firing of my brother's .243 Winchester Savage. It destroyed all pretense, and the family was divided into two camps. The line was drawn. Mom versus Dad. My Brother and Sister on one side, and I, my Father's son, on the other. Alone. And ruthless. My mind, obsessed with doing what was right, believed it was "right" that Taylor Gordon sing. And so he sang.

My Dad never met a God he didn't like. The God of the Jews, the Christians, the Hindus, the Muslims, the Sufis; the God of the Sun, the Corn; the God of Sunsets and Sunrises, of Dewy Spring Mornings, of Music and Laughter . . . he loved them all. Bring him the Supreme Being in any shape or form and he would embrace it. Religion, on the other hand, he treated with disdain. He had little use for the middlemen. He believed we were all our own best connection to the Infinite, and he loathed any kind of organized or institutionalized religion. So when it came to his funeral, I knew a church was out of the question. There would be a brief ceremony at the funeral home, owned by his good friend Kenny Twichell, then the whole act would move to the local Castle Mountain Cemetery and conclude under the Big Sky of Montana.

At the Twichell Funeral Home, I sat with the family while Rose Gordon played the organ and Taylor sang my Dad's favorite song. An obscure, ridiculously romantic love song from the 1920s, of a beautiful young girl and a young man's unrequited love for her. It was called "Sylvia." Whenever my Dad sang it, which he did at least once a week while accompanying himself on the piano, I always had the strangely disturbing impression that the beautiful young girl of the song represented that finest part of himself he felt was lost and gone forever. And for which he pined eternally. It must have struck the members of the funeral party as a disturbing and strange choice. Taylor Gordon's rendition, sung with the rich passion of the operatic baritone Ringling Brother's Circus had paid to train, was glorious and moving beyond words. It confused the hell out of all but the closest friends. I knew the convoluted paradox of a black man's interpretation of a teenage love song from the 1920s, being sung in the 1960s for a white man's funeral, would have pleased my Dad to no end. "Always keep 'em guessing."

Our little family tragedy made all the Montana papers. The coroner's inquest had decided self-defense. But murder was the murmur that drove word of mouth. My Dad was a very well-known attorney. He had the kind of friends and enemies that come with integrity—all loyal. Many of them came to the funeral. In those days, you had to be there. You couldn't wait to catch it on "Oprah," "Donahue," "Sally Jessy," or "Geraldo." It made for an interesting mix. The ceremony was brief, the situation volatile. Everybody knew too much and too little and the less said the better.

The family didn't carpool on its way to the cemetery. I had, in my determination to be loyal to my Father, decided to drive to the cemetery separately that I might let the "world" know that there was more going on there than met the eye.

I hadn't read or acted him yet, but I understood Hamlet too well. Would that I had had his words to explain the behavior that to the world seemed so strange:

> Seems, Madam! Nay, it is. I know not "seems."
> 'Tis not alone my inky cloak . . .
> Nor customary suits of solemn black . . .
> Nor the dejected havior of the visage,
> Together with all forms, moods, shows of grief,
> That can denote me truly. These indeed seem,
> For they are actions that a man might play.
> But I have that within which passeth show,
> These but the trappings and the suits of woe.

Upon leaving the funeral home for the short drive to the cemetery where my Father would be buried, my Mother's lawyer tried to drag me into the car where my Mother, Brother, and Sister sat waiting. A scuffle erupted in front *of the members of the funeral party. Kenny Twichell put a stop to this embarrassing tussle. I was "allowed" to do as I wished. I rode the two miles to the beautiful Castle Mountain Cemetery with a friend of my Father who knew the family dynamics, knew I was odd son out, and had contacted me the day after my Dad was shot to offer assistance. My Mother, Brother, and Sister rode in one car. I rode in another. It would be the beginning of my life's unshared journey as my Father's ambassador to the world. Alone with the terrible responsibility of carrying on his unfulfilled dreams and ambitions. "To be or not to be . . ." became my life's question. To do or not to do, to accomplish or not to accomplish, to live up to or not to live up to the life I felt was my responsibility to realize.*

Burying the dead is so much easier when you don't know them. When they are not of your flesh. And spirit. Earlier that summer, while my Dad was having his last days on Earth, though probably not enjoying them, I had worked briefly as assistant caretaker of the Castle Mountain Cemetery. I tended the dead. Mowed and watered the ten acres of beautiful grass, trimmed around the headstones, weeded the flowers, and even dug two graves during the time I worked there. The people who visited were always very appreciative of how well you maintained the final resting place of their dearly departed. I was, in fact, making almost as much in tips as I was in salary. My Dad was temporarily (oh, so temporarily) living in a local motel and would sometimes visit me at work. A restraining order kept him 100 feet from the family home. What was 100 feet or 1,000 feet compared to the measureless emotional chasm that had years before distanced him from his family? But he was considered dangerous, and the law, in its wisdom, deemed 100 feet a "safe" distance. But there is no law that can keep a man from his children. No law that can keep us safe from ourselves and the drama, trauma, of our own lives. The only restraining order that would keep him from anything, including his own salvation, was not legal but ballistic. And though it accomplished many things, it did not render any of us safe. For he was, his spirit was, destined to haunt us all.

The cemetery where I worked was on the outskirts of town and well beyond the 100-foot radius of the family domicile, past which my Father could not pass, legally, and he would visit me there during my lunch break. We would sit among the dead and discuss the dilemmas of the living over the venison sausage sandwiches and tea that my Mother prepared daily for me. How horribly apropos that we should have so many of our final Father-and-Son talks in the land of the dead. We both knew that time was running out for us. But what we didn't know was that time was running out for him. Forever.

I loved the job. The work was easy, the environment peaceful and serene. Peace and serenity, qualities woefully lacking in my existence. I particularly enjoyed the gravedigging, as it provided an opportunity to build muscle for football. I was soon, August 18, to play in the annual East-West Football Game, a game honoring the best high school football players in the state. I was the first player from White Sulphur Springs to be so honored. My Dad was singularly proud of this accomplishment. We discussed it at length and he helped me keep it and my future college football career in perspective during our graveyard chats.

How strange it was to be in my former place of employment standing by my Dad's grave. Not waiting, with professional decorum, to fill it in, but waiting, in abject fear, to mourn its filling. My Father and I once again, and for the last time, side by side by graveside. And I can still hear him talking, putting even this experience into perspective. But I can't listen. How far, far away seemed the eighteen-year-old of weeks before to this eighteen-year-old postmortem adult. The innocence of youth lost in the violence of death, in the fraction of the hair-triggered second that separates them. Life (and death) is full of surprises. But was this really? I felt in my heart that I had, with the pick and shovel of broken promises, also dug my Father's grave. I couldn't see that he had spent his life digging his own grave. That his life was nothing more than preparation for this moment. That how we "do" decides how we are "undone." Restraining orders and high-powered hunting rifles are neither the causes nor the cures, but simply allopathic treatments of systemic diseases of dysfunction.

Being a professional gravedigger, I appreciated the clean, neatly squared corners of the grave dug by my former grave-digging partner. I could see, with my expert eye, that extra care had been taken. Maybe I should tip him? Did he lurk back in the trees, as we had done, waiting for the ceremony to be over and the tearful mourners to depart before we moved in with our sharp shovels and black humor? Would he climb onto my Father's casket (that had always been my task) to jostle it into position before burying it forever with the rich soil of Montana? I was overcome with the desire to remain behind after the brief graveside cere-mony, pick up a shovel, and bury my Father. Really bury my Father. If this was a rite of passage, I believed that only this act could get me to the other shore. For I had yet to believe in ghosts and thought where my Father's body went he went, too. I now know it didn't matter. That I couldn't shovel my way free. That this was not the end it appeared to be but only the beginning. My Father was still very much with me. Perhaps more than ever, as he was now free of any and all "restraining orders" and could follow me wherever, forever. Through all my waking, sleeping nightmares and dreams. I didn't believe in ghosts. How could I exorcise them?

I gazed on the distant mountains where I had spent my youth, much of it in the company of my Father. Everything disappeared. There was no priest, no gathering of friends and not-so friends kissing and hugging their condolences, no tortured Brother and Sister with their own lives of dysfunc-tion stretching before them, no lurking gravedigger. Noth-ing except the distant horizon and the beckoning of my heart's yearning to be free. I believed I would survive. Little did I know how little I knew.

My kindred spirit, Hamlet, speaks to me:

And a man's life's no more than to say "One."

And I feel the lid to my coffin being lifted. Toni shakes me. What happened? Is everything okay? Why is Toni walking around? Why is she waking me? I climb out of my coffin. Shake away the ghosts. Of Hamlet. Of Father's past.

"Darling, can you come? She keeps falling asleep."

"She?" I ask. "What time is it?" Another contraction begins. Toni sighs at the inevitability of it all and heads back to the bedroom. I glance at the clock . . . it is 1:00 in the morning! And a man's life's no more than to say "One."

Moonlight spills through the second-story window of my study, where I have been sleeping. Dreaming. I am drawn to it . . . *the Ghost of Father's Past*. With sleepy anticipation I look out on the four acres that surround this 1930s-style farmhouse. I see the fruit orchard, the tack barn, the 7,000-gallon holding tank for our well; the newly built tennis court, my Ford pickup—I see it all in the irradiate glow of moonlight. Not a ghost in sight.

Burying the dead and birthing the living are opposite sides of the same thin coin we call life. We are born into the visible world. We die into the invisible. Maybe it doesn't work that way. Maybe we've got it backwards. Maybe we die when we are born, and are born when we die. Born into the infinite world from the finite. If infinity was yours, would you settle for less? Birth. Death. Misnomers for our endless transformation from one to the other. Was my Father's violent home death the equivalent of the murderous medical marvel of cesarean birth? The surgeon's knife rips us into "this" world. The hunting rifle's bullet takes us (him) into the "next." Sans segue. Brutal spiritual transformation. Damaged auras. Mangled karma. Astrological charts knocked askew. How many generations, how many reincarnations will it take to make amends with the Order of the Universe? How many ghosts from cesarean deaths and births hover in a state of spiritual limbo? Et tu, Brute?

I enter the bedroom. Something is wrong. Toni sits on one side of the bed; the "professional" reclines on the other. My little snack must have really hit the spot because she's sleeping like the baby we are desperately trying to have. Upon my departure for a much-needed nap, the attendant lay down on the bed, presumably to rub Toni's lower back, and went promptly to sleep. Toni has been alone all this time! She didn't want to wake me because she knew how tired I was. Toni tried moaning a little louder than normal during contractions to rouse the pro, but evidently Grandma's party was very tiring.

Toni has a contraction. I let my voice project as I begin to coach her through it. (After all, I am a classically trained stage actor. I know how to reach the balcony.) Lo and behold, the Rip Van Winkle of home births raises her sleepy head from her pillow. I'm embarrassed for her. She isn't. She seems quite content with herself, unfazed by her lack of professionalism in going to sleep on the job. If this were the military and she a sentry, she would be shot. I consider that option. She better not ask for dessert! She's fortunate that I'm too tired and busy taking care of Toni to do anything but ignore her. She ignores us! Is she waiting for me to tell her what I want her to do? Evidently not. She goes downstairs. That is, after all, where the refrigerator is. Is this a raid? I feel a tinge of anger. Let it pass. It is important that Toni has nothing to distract her from what she is going through. Her energy must be conserved for the coming event. And when is that going to be? I must maintain a calm and serene atmosphere for Toni. My anxieties must not become hers. Well, we have gone it alone this far; we shall just continue.

Toni's courage, stamina, and humor give me a second wind. Good thing, because it is now 1:30 in the morning, the next morning, Sunday, February 28, 1988. Twenty-five hours of labor. Hard labor.

Sunday? I lost my Father on a Sunday. August 4, 1963. Twenty-five years ago. Twenty-five years of labor. Hard labor. Giving birth to this moment?

Chapter Nine

I t isn't easy. It is never easy. Nor is it meant to be. None of it. Not birth, not death, and certainly not life. I was born in 1945. I've been around awhile. I can remember things. It gives me pause.

I remember that somewhere in the 1960s women got fed up, had had enough. They burned their bras, bought their birth control pills, and demanded their sexual freedom. They wanted sex the way men had always had it. Casual. Without love, without responsibility, without procreation. Just another sporting event. They wanted it and they got it. I remember this. Do you? Sleeping with someone didn't mean you wanted to have his child! That mindset had ruined their mothers' lives, and by God and the grace of modern chemistry, it was not about to ruin theirs! Or to stop them from reaching those baby-free multiple orgasms that they had heard were theirs for the taking. As part of their redefined feminine destiny. Men enjoyed sex for sex's sake, and come hell or high sperm count, so would they. What was good for the gander was going to be much better for the goose. Needless to say, singles bars became very in, birth control manufacturers got very rich, and lots of grateful guys got laid.

But there were forces at work here that went beyond man- and womankind's ideas of what was "right," and women began to sense that all the screwing around they were doing wasn't worth all the screwing around they were getting. Multiple orgasms remained, for most, something to read about in *Cosmo* and seldom experience in eros. All the "good" men were taken. And all men, the good, the bad, and the ugly (if rich), were no longer interested in them for anything except . . . surprise, surprise, surprise . . . sex! Do you remember this? I do. I lived it. Sex. For a night or a week or maybe a couple of months, and then all of us, the-good-the-bad-and-the-ugly, excused ourselves into the sexual marketplace to find another liberated female. What was good for the goose was feeling very, very good for the gander. Sex was everywhere. Women were discovering what men already knew. Once you start, you can never stop. Variety was no longer simply the spice of life; it became a way of life. Things were very much out of everyone's control. Would it never end? Of course. But only when enough had become far, far too much.

The libido may have been willing, but the body became weak. It was called herpes. A strange little virus for which, alas, there was no cure. No magic bullet. It struck fear into the hearts of everyone, especially the owners of the swinging singles bars. Horrible. "Sixty Minutes" even did a segment on this terrible disease. Do you remember this? I do. I also remember that, as Mother Nature would have it, herpes would be swept from the papers, from the minds of singles-bar owners, even from the airwaves of "Sixty Minutes." Swept into a footnote in the history of social diseases along with venereal disease, gonorrhea, and yeast infection. Swept into obscurity by the sexual party pooper to end all party poopers ... AIDS!

AIDS. The final nail in the coffin in which would be buried (forever?) the planetary promiscuity that had run rampant for decades. The Sexual Revolution, which had begun in the 1960s at the bequest of women who dreamed of freedom, ended in the 1980s in despair and loneliness.

It was time to reflect. Only Father Time, women were shocked to discover, was running out on them. (Isn't that just like a man?) Women who were in their early twenties when they declared their sexual freedom were now in their late thirties. Time flies when you're having orgasms. And now, after years of listening to the sisterhood talk of feminine equality, she began to hear a different kind of talk. "Tick-tock" talk. Biological clock . . . talk. With each year, each month, each week, it became louder and louder and finally so loud that it drowned out every other thought she ever had. Her birth control pills had given her menstrual relationships in lieu of menstrual cycles; her liberation had given her sexual freedom; her orgasms have given her ... orgasms. But none of this had given her what she really wanted. Her mother was laughing. Grandma rolled over in her grave. And the clock kept ticking. . . . Tick-talk . . . ba-by. Tick-talk . . . ba-by. Tick-talk . . . *ba-by!*

Women always get what they want, which is how we got into this situation in the first place. So they got their babies.

Started having them left and right. With husbands, with boyfriends, with syringes; and if their biological clock was too abused or run down to have babies, they hired other, younger, healthier women to have the babies for them. Motherhood by proxy. And they thanked the "miracle" of modern medicine, always on the lookout for a way to circumvent Mother Nature, for giving them what they had sought so passionately for decades to avoid. What they had avoided at all costs, they would now have at all costs. Have their cake and eat it too. Abort their fetus and have it too.

During the sexual revolution, we believed that sex was possible without commitment. That physical promiscuity didn't mean mental, emotional, spiritual promiscuity. That we could give our bodies and keep our souls. That when we became diseased physically, we didn't necessarily become diseased, scarred, or damned emotionally, mentally, or spiritually. That modern medicine would cure our physical diseases so we could continue our promiscuous ways. Then, with herpes, things began to unravel. No cure. Terrible, but you didn't die from it. But things unraveled some more . . . AIDS. But that's the "H" disease. Only homosexuals, Haitians, and heroin addicts die from it. Then we realized that heterosexual is also an "H" word, and we began to discover that the moral fabric of America is much looser than anyone ever dreamed. The immune system of America is much weaker than your doctor will (can) tell you. And AIDS is more deadly and widespread than anyone imagined. The bubble, at long last, burst. And truth, in spite of ourselves, was out.

Have we learned anything? Or are we only readjusting our self-centered lifestyles till modern medicine comes up with the magic potion that will do to HIV what penicillin did to venereal disease and gonorrhea? What the pill did to the menstrual cycle? What air conditioning did to the heat wave? Do we still worship false gods? Do we still think man-womankind controls the Universe? That we are not responsible for our dread diseases? That a disease of the body is not a disease of the spirit? That we can swing like the Jims of Baker and Swaggart and still be "spiritual" leaders? That surrogate parenting is free from spiritual ramifications, that sperm banks carry no karmic consequences? Are we still betting on modern science to forgive us our sins and save our souls?

With our hospitals full of the sick and dying; with moral degeneration evident in every segment of our society; with child abuse and molestation increasing, our prisons full to overflowing, our family's destiny in the hands of corporate America; with our children overfed and undernourished, overweight and undereducated—with all this and an endless list of further agonies, is it not time to change direction? To travel not further out but further in? To spend not more but less? To eat not out but in?

Isn't the tick-talk of our bio-eco-logical clock telling us, possibly for the last time, that it is time to just stay home? And accept, finally and forever, total responsibility for all our crimes against the Universe?

Which is to say, against ourselves?

Chapter Ten

Where was I? Drifting. Remembering how I got here, trying to see where I'm going. I know. I'm going to call Jackie. The contractions are growing more intense; the birth attendant is downstairs, probably raiding the refrigerator. Who knows? Who cares? I have had enough. I am going to call Jackie and bring her little soirée to an end.

I call the hotel. Tell them it is an emergency and they should find Jackie the Black-Belt Midwife immediately and have her call me. I consider telling them that I am an actor and used to be (before "The A-Team" was canceled) a TV star. I think better of it.

My experience has been that I only get recognized when I don't want to be. Chances are that the guy on the other end of the phone has never heard of me or "The A-Team" and I'll have to start down the long list of my credits in hopes that he recognizes *something* I've been in. And if he doesn't, I'm worse off than if I'd just kept my quasi-famous mouth shut. These and other thoughts flit through my mind as I wait for her to call back, which she does in about twenty minutes.

I inform her how unprofessional her professional birth attendant has been. "Not to worry," she says. She sounds very calm. Maybe she's found her beeper? She tells me she has a friend who has helped her with numerous births. She'll give her a call.

"But what if she isn't available?" I ask with the experience of the snake-bitten.

"Oh, she's available. She wanted to come in the first place, but I had promised someone else." The one with sleeping sickness, I wonder? My God! People have been auditioning for the, as yet uncast, part of attendant to my, as yet unborn, baby's birth. Maybe I'm a bigger star than I thought? Maybe the show is in reruns? Maybe I'm losing my mind? Never mind. Back to business.

I say yes to Jackie's second choice for the part of Birth Attendant. Do I have a choice? What the hell, if she can stay away from Disneyland, away from food, and awake, she'll be a vast improvement.

"When can you get here?" I ask.

"How is Toni? How far apart are the contractions?" she asks.

Toni's a rock, superwoman; the contractions are about the same but a little longer in duration. Is she avoiding the question?

"When can you get here?" I ask. Again.

"Soon," she says. Is she avoiding the question? "Okay, I'll leave the party and head your way in about half an hour."

Not soon enough as far as I'm concerned. Hasn't she got Chuck Norris's autograph yet? She says she'll be at our place around 3:00 a.m., and the new birthing attendant will arrive first thing in the morning. First thing in whose morning? As far as I'm concerned it is the first thing in the morning. I'm losing my grip. I hang up.

By 3:00 a.m. we will have been in labor twenty-seven hours! Just the two of us. Toni and I. For better or for worse. In sickness and in health. In pregnancy and in birth. Till the damn baby is born. Or death do us part.

I don't know about birth (I'm about to learn), but I do know about death. And death do us *not* part. If birth is the appetizer and life the main course, then death . . . death is dessert. It can be the perfect ending to a much-enjoyed feast or the dreaded, irresistible, unavoidable, exquisitely agonizing moment when you face all your worst fears about yourself. It is the final piece in the puzzle, the last taste in the smorgasbord of life. After dessert, after death, the oblivion of . . . sleep? I think not.

My Father's dessert may have been on his karmic menu, but it was not what he wanted, not in the moment that it was presented to him. I know. I was there.

"Put the gun down." That's what he said. But the moment was out of control. Beyond his control. Beyond anyone's control. Except mine? Except mine? The moment was spinning, spinning, spinning out of control. If only I had seized the moment. The rifle. But it wasn't my life on the line. I had other needs, other cravings to be satisfied. But the

muzzle swings in my direction and I think it is my life on the line. But that was after, after the moment. After he says, "Oh, my God . . . No!"

How can he say that, how can he say anything after being shot from a distance of five feet? And with such heart-rending accuracy?

And after the dessert of death it is time for guilt. For denial. For wishing it all away. Why? Why? But death does not us part, and my Father's dessert becomes the main course of my life.

I can see that now. I couldn't see it then. Why not? I was there. I was there and yet I couldn't see it. I was there and yet I wasn't there.

On that final Sunday morning, my Father left me standing in the backyard and made his final plunge into the swirling waters of family failure. He knew where he was going. Not to meet his maker. Nor to face the seething, blonde-haired, blue-eyed rage of his twenty-four-year-old, first-born manchild. But to finish what had begun with the most complex sentence ever uttered by any man: "I do." It had taken twenty-six years, but he knew where he was going and it was to the bedroom of their shattered bliss. He knew she'd be waiting for him. He should have known he was overmatched, had been forever and always.

Shattered vows, shattered dreams, shattered lives. Bloody, shattered window in the back door of the family home, betraying his forced entry. Forcing himself back into the family that had forced him out. Forcing the moment to its crisis. Throwing caution to the wind, life down the drain.

His restraining order waits in the hallway to the bed-

room where she sleeps and where he heads, in his final kamikaze plunge toward brutal consummation of the marriage vows they made twenty-six years before. "I do" becomes "I will!"

When they met, my Mother was twenty, a beautiful farm girl from north of Havre, struck by my Father's vitality (as she soon will be again) and his brilliance. He was twenty-six, blinded by her beauty and ignorant of his own strange, unshared dreams of a life no one had heard of or cared to know or believed was possible.

"I do," he said. And it would take him twenty-six years, but, by God and in spite of what he must have known was waiting, he would.

"Till death do us part," he said. But death parts only the spirit from the body. It leaves all the conflict, rage, fear, and resentment just where they were—in the hearts and minds of the living.

My heart and mind resist, but my body follows my Father. I leave the backyard where we stood and follow the trail of his rage. To the back door of the house, through the shattered window of forced entry. Forced entry into the future and the bedroom and the blur that would become Me. I have followed him ever since. Through other shattered dreams and bloody broken windows of opportunity. Through heartbreak and carcinogenic nightmares.

In 1955, my parents built on to our house a large living (dying) room. More room for happiness? Or less room for error? (Alas, happiness is not measured in square feet.) It was a simple addition. One large room attached to the front with four huge bay windows that looked out onto the Castle

Mountains thirty miles to the east (giving us the same view as the cemetery). Big fireplace at one end. Swivel chairs in front of the windows so you could sit there and look either out on the mountain scenery or in on the family tragedy. We mostly looked out. Spotting elk with our Army-issued binoculars, then piling into our '48 Willy's Jeep and driving up to hunt them with our high-powered hunting rifles.

This large front living room gave us space to wrestle and dance and play games and open Christmas presents in front of the fire. In the front room in front of the fire with the unfolding tragedy in the back, behind the smoldering familial fires. Way in the back, behind the laughter and the wrestling and the piano recitals. But in the back is not where my Father was shot. It is where we lived and where he died but not where he was shot.

The bullet came from the front. Did he see it coming? Did any of us? Didn't we all? But what could we do? Some things are just not said. Not until it's too late.

"Put the gun down," he says, facing my Brother in the hallway. And again, "Put the gun down."

But the gun goes off, not down. And the muzzle swings. And I go not toward my Father but away. A blur into the front room. Not toward but away. Did I think I was saving myself?

I go into the simple addition that is our front living room. My Mother sits on the bay window seat by the fireplace. She turns her battered face to me. Did I go to her? Have I yet to go to her? Does she still sit, in pain, on her Big Sky window seat waiting for her younger son to come to her? To make it all better? She is a blur. It is all a blur . . . past, present, future

. . . a blur. I am in her womb, in her arms, on her knee . . .
all a blur. My Brother is on the phone, calling someone he
knows who is an officer of the peace. Peace on Earth? A
blur. Goodwill toward men? A blur. Toward Father?

"Bill, you better come up to the house. I just shot my
Dad." All a blur.

I'm running now. Standing still in the big front room
but running in my mind. Looking for escape, for elk in the
Castle Mountains. Looking, my Father alive and at my side,
for blue grouse in the Park Hills, for trout in the Smith River,
for focus in the moment. For anything. Except revenge. We
always hunted. Yes, always. But with each other, never for.
Never!

Or did we always hunt for nothing but one another? For
what we, as a family, had lost. For what we had. Once. A Father,
Mother, Daughter, and two Sons, all hunting for their husband, wife, son, daughter, brother, sister. Is predestined mem-
bership in the Parenticide Club the fate of all misunderstood
children?

If this is so, I don't want it. Don't want fatherhood. Don't
want this child that will haunt me to my grave with its constant
reminder of my failure and the failure of my Father and all
fathers past. But wait. It is already too late for that. I am a
father. For fatherhood is not a state of place but of mind, and
my mind has long since left the simple addition of the added
front room of my shattered Big Sky childhood.

Will I force my children's hands? There must be another
way. Can I not bury my Father's ghost? Give him the freedom
he has sought so long, even before he plunged through the

glass of the back door. Sought for all eternity. Is that not my, any son's, duty?

Sons arise. Set your fathers free.

And when that Last Sunday Supper comes, oh fathers, what will be your just desserts?

The hours come. The hours go. The contractions come. The contractions go. How long before Jackie gets here? The phone rings. I hesitate. No, I must. The last thing I need now is somebody's unsolicited help.

"Hello, is Toni there?" Oh boy, is she!

"Who's calling?" I ask curtly.

"This is Carol." Carol? The voice continues, "Rhonda was killed this afternoon in a motorcycle accident." The voice collapses in on itself, sobbing uncontrollably.

I am stunned. My mind, too much with thoughts of the dead in this trial by birth, struggles to find room for yet one more ghost. Rhonda? Rhonda? And I remember. She is one of Toni's best friends from elementary school. Carol's sobs continue, the tears of motherhood. I haven't the words, the energy, the emotional reserve to deal with what this moment calls for. I am speechless. I look through the window.

The orchard is bathed in moonlight. I envy her tears. I have yet to shed mine. Two people, strangers, with only death in common. She cries uncontrollably over the death of her child. I struggle to maintain control as I face the birth of mine, the death of my Father. I try to find the words. I have yet to find the tears. Words are beyond hope. I can't tell her that death is not the end, that maybe she is one of the lucky ones and her daughter's ghost will not haunt her. I can't tell her what I want to know. I hang onto the phone in silence and I can feel her, too, hanging on. Life and death and nothing but Pacific Bell in between.

"Toni isn't here right now, Carol. I'll tell her as soon as she gets in." Lies, lies, lies.

Through the sobbing I hear, "Thank you so much."

No, don't thank me. I have done nothing. I did nothing for my Father then. I have done nothing for you now. There is a click. Sobs become silence.

I hang up the phone. Take one last look outside. The moon has disappeared behind storm clouds. All is black. All is not well. Unless it ends well. Where is Hamlet when I need him?

> *. . . we defy augury. There's a special*
> *providence in the fall of a sparrow. If it*
> *be now, 'tis not to come; if it be not to come,*
> *it will be now; if it be not now, yet it will come.*
> *The readiness is all. . . . Let be.*

I go back to Toni.

"Who was that?" she asks.

"Steve. He wants to know how it's going."

It is important her mind be filled only with life and the giving of it. Let Carol and me have our deadly secrets. Time enough to tell the truth.

Toni has gone without sleep for over a day, and I worry how long it will be before she weakens. Loses her faith. Faith. Without it we are lost.

Was Toni's decision to have this birth at home her own? Or was it loving acquiescence to my own faith in the natural correctness of it? Merely submission to my own fanatical belief, born in the death of my Father, that the instant the bullet is released from its barrel, the infant from its womb, the path they will follow is irrevocable? Does she believe, as I do, that in our birth lies the crucial creation of the trajectory of our life and, finally, our death?

Home births are considered primitive by most. Certainly by all our friends, who thought we were mad to even consider it. How could we turn our backs on all the marvelous advances of medical science and return to the witchcraft of midwives and home births? But then medical so-called science is not the god I pay homage to, and "primitive" is not a bad word in my dictionary. I long for a more primitive existence for myself and the world. Intellectuals be damned!

Ever since mankind began its worship of the mind, with the absolute faith that it is indeed totally separate from the body and spirit and the answer to all mankind's hopes and dreams, ever since then, which goes back centuries, and then some, we have scoffed at the primordial beliefs of the primitives. With each passing century, the primitive cultures of the world have dwindled in number until they now exist only in pitiful disappearing pockets of simplicity. All for the sake of civilization.

True to the form of this so-called civilized world, they will become extinct at exactly the same time we realize that they were right. All along and about everything.

The one common thread in all their cultures is their absolute faith in the connective consciousness of all things. They know body, mind, and spirit not as three, not separate, but as one. The primitive mind recognizes the spiritual aspect of all things. It worships the same gods of my Father's eccentric mind: the sun god, corn god, gods of the sea, of the trees, of the fishes. Nothing is excluded. They believe that their health and happiness depends on the health and happiness of all things. How childish. How silly. How true.

I never laughed at these notions when my Father first espoused them. But I did learn to keep my primitive thoughts to myself when later, in college, I heard these cultures described as heathen and savage and was taught that the real and logical gods were Aristotle, Socrates, and the ilk of their analytical kind. I was coerced to place my primitive instinct for survival in the hands of the gods of science and accept planetary pollution (extinction) as the necessary byproduct of progress. I learned to keep my minority opinions and my Father's words to myself.

Chapter Eleven

I don't have the heart (the courage?) to tell Toni that one of her closest friends has been killed. Not now. We move through the next four hours as we have passed through the previous twenty-four, in little bits and chunks of three and five minutes. The ritual of birth. The part they never show you in the movies. Toni contracts while I soothe and comfort. She then rests, waiting for the next while I hurry off to check the food that is forever cooking downstairs in the kitchen or run the hot bath she has every hour.

The doorbell rings. I look at the clock: 4:00 a.m. Jackie has arrived. Finally. She looks tired. Partying will do that to you. I vaguely remember those days. They were tough, but compared to this? . . . a piece of cake. Jackie slips out of Toni's party dress (wonder if Chuck held it in his arms?) and slips into her work clothes. A sartorial segue from man catching to baby catching.

The baby's heartbeat is a reflection of its momma. Strong and steady. Everything is fine. Except Toni is only about six and a half centimeters dilated! Not good news. Given the strength and length of Toni's contractions and the number of hours she has been having them, she should be close to the ten centimeters of full dilation. We are, however, a long way from the magic number ten. Never, outside the world of Carl Lewis, has three and a half centimeters seemed such a long, long way to go.

Jackie puts on a pair of disposable rubber gloves. They snap loudly as she pulls them snugly onto her hands. Toni contracts while Jackie manipulates the cervix with her hand in an attempt to help the process of dilation. Just how she massages, manipulates, I can only imagine. How it feels to Toni is beyond imagining. I look on in wonder. I can tell it isn't pleasant for Toni. But it is working. I feel like a cervical auctioneer.

"We got six and a half, how 'bout a seven? Seven come eleven. Settle for ten. Six and a half come ten. Okay, seven! Give me a seven, seven, what d'ya say, seven?" Not much action. Wait a minute. Seven! "We got seven. Gimme an eight." And on and on to myself.

Eight doesn't come, but after another half hour, seven and a half centimeters. And then another hour and finally eight! Now we're getting someplace. Only two more centimeters to go.

The final two centimeters of cervical dilation are called Transition. The most difficult stage of labor. The contractions become very, very strong and last sometimes as long as a minute and a half. Fortunately, it is also the shortest phase of labor, lasting usually no more than thirty to forty-five minutes.

Toni is eight centimeters dilated. We're getting close. Why do I feel we have such a long way to go? Maybe it's the blood? There is blood everywhere.

It would be the first of what seemed to be gallons of blood that I would see before we were through. Reminds me of my carnivorous youth when I hunted, killed, and cleaned the deer, ducks, grouse, pheasants, and other warm-blooded animals of Montana. Blood! Birthing babies is bloody business. I wonder where it all comes from?

The blood of birth. The blood of death. I know where my Father's came from and saw where it went: on the bedroom wall. All over my Mother's wallpaper. Who cleaned it off? Who cleaned up that and other bloodier messes from that day? It wasn't me. I know that. It wasn't me. Perhaps it's not too late?

The rubber glove continues it's snap, snap, snap as it disappears, massages, reappears . . . snap! Disappear, massage, reappear, snap! Disappear, massage, reappear, snap! I am about to snap! How does Toni endure? Always I wonder this . . . how can she endure this unimaginable test of physical conditioning? Test of faith.

I bring her food. All my bachelor years of cooking come in handy. I realize her energy depends on my food. It is my one tangible involvement in the birth of our child. The only way I can get inside this closed circle of mother and child. My cooking, my food, becomes Toni's blood, becomes, via its umbilical connection to her, the blood of our child.

Toni and I have been eating well for years in preparation

for this event. Long before the child was conceived. How strange that couples get so concerned with smoking and with drinking coffee and alcohol when they become pregnant, while for months, years, prior to conception they eat and drink with total disregard. Like training for a marathon race long after it has started. At what point do we take responsibility for the quality of the children we are going to have? At what point does parenthood begin?

It begins at the beginning. Every "thing" we are, every thought we think, every food we eat . . . physical, mental, and spiritual . . . become our children. This is the real legacy we leave them, the constitution they inherit, the genetic code that will dictate the direction of their lives. Alcoholic parents have alcoholic babies. Crack parents have crack babies. Meat-and-sugar parents have meat-and-sugar babies. Fast-food junkies procreate fast-food junkies. We are born with the addictions, the lifestyles, the genes of our parents. Our destiny lies not in our stars but in our genes. It is inevitable. It is in our blood!

I cook Toni's food. I wipe her brow. I mop up blood. I run errands for Jackie. And I worry. With the passage of time, bloody thoughts, and countless rubber gloves, Toni is still only eight centimeters dilated. We are close. But not getting closer.

The baby is still very strong but has not descended; that is, its head has not engaged with the cervix. This is one of the reasons for the slowness of dilation. It is important that the baby's head descends as it puts pressure on the cervix and assists in the effacing (thinning) and dilation of the cervix. The position of our baby is right occiput anterior, meaning its head is on Toni's right side facing her left hip. It refuses to rotate into the correct position for birth, which is facing down, or back toward the mother's spine, with its head engaged. Jackie had hoped once Toni was fully dilated she could get the baby to move into the correct position. So far, no good.

Toni has been working hard for several hours. Jackie is running low on rubber gloves. Things are at a standstill. Jackie suggests a walk. The fresh air and movement of a walk may do Toni some good. I look at Toni. Having this baby is what would do her good. She's ready to try anything.

It is 45°F outside. I help Toni put on some warm clothes. This goes very slowly as it must be accomplished between contractions. Finally we are ready. It will be the first time Toni has been outside since Friday, a day and a lifetime ago.

The moon is full. Clouds scoot across it. Rain falls intermittently. The wind blows enough to create atmosphere but not enough to create wind chill. It is magic. We hold hands and stroll through our orchard. Peach trees, apple trees, plum trees, nectarine trees, pear trees . . . all, like Toni, in full bloom. The moonlight reflects off the petals. The wind rustles everything. The rain rinses the strain from my face.

Toni has a contraction. She squats under a blossoming Japanese Plum tree and moans in the moonlight. Our two-and-a-half-year-old Akbash named Kazi (short for Kamikaze) joins us. He is a Turkish guard dog, and his guarding instincts are aroused by the sight and sound of Toni's travail. He nuzzles her. Toni strokes his pure white coat. It glows in the moonlight. He follows and nuzzles as we walk and squat. Walk, squat, nuzzle. Walk, squat, nuzzle. With each contraction, Toni holds onto my hands as she hunches down. Occasionally I lean over, my hands on my knees, and Toni uses me for support as she bends across my back and breathes through the contractions. They come as they have always come, like waves crashing on a rocky shore—endless, relentless, inescapable. Three to five minutes apart and forty-five seconds in duration. Every now and then there will be one that is very intense and we will think this is it, the beginning of Transition; our moonlit stroll has done the trick. But then the next will be less severe, and we continue our moonwalk with our faithful Kazi in protective attendance. Nuzzling and guarding. He is only one generation removed from the wildness of his native Turkey, where he guarded mother sheep and their lambs from coyotes. His instincts have yet to be bred out of him by American breeders interested only in winning awards at dog shows. He knows what we are going through. It is in his blood. I wish I could tell him how much he comforts us. Perhaps he knows that, too.

Since this home birth began, I have been timing everything with my stopwatch. I time contractions, both their duration and the time in between. I time how long between baths, how long since Toni last ate, how long since Jackie called, how long since it all began. I time everything. I have become obsessed with time. And in my obsession with time, I have also lost track of it, of what time it actually is. I time how long since we came outside. Don't want to overdo it. How can you overdo a labor that has already lasted nearly thirty hours? How can you overdo what is in the hands of Mother Nature?

We continue our stroll through the orchard. Moonbeams surround us. Romance and poetry shrouded in mystery. The moon, the clouds, the wind, and the rain mix and swirl. Magic.

"Right out of a movie," I tell Toni.

She laughs, "You've been in show business too long." But

she agrees. We couldn't have asked for more terrible, wonderful, unforgettable weather. (As if we could ever forget any of this!) Southern California may be famous for its lack of meteorological variety, but not this weekend. No sir, there is definitely something in the air. We are not alone. I look for ghosts.

My father! Methinks I see my father!

He has been with us all along, now bathed in moonlight, watching us squat and walk and nuzzle. Waiting to see. What? If I would get it? That nothing is more important to us than whom we choose to love and marry and beget? I want to introduce him to Toni. "Whatever you do, Son, don't marry the wrong woman." He should know that I didn't. Or does he? How long has he been there? I remember him dying, I can't remember him leaving. Maybe now? Maybe with the birth of his grandchild? Is that why you never left? Because you didn't get it right. And now you are waiting to see. . . .
"If it's a girl, it's Hannah. If it's a boy, it's you. George."
The second coming of George. Maybe then?

Toni nudges me. Kazi nuzzles me. The moon disappears. It is time to go in. To leave the ghosts of Father's past and the magic of our fruitful stroll down moonlit dreams of a future full of children.

I am, for the first time in hours, overcome with the feeling that everything is going to be all right. That this rite of passage is right on schedule. We are learning something, and the child that is on its way, kicking up a storm inside its momma's belly, is also kicking up a storm outside its momma's belly for a reason. If so, it certainly has our attention. Nothing exists for me but the child and its mother, my wife. Shall it always be thus? Will nothing really count for me, from this time hence, except my wife and children?

Chapter Twelve

Toni and I come in out of the cold eager to find out if ambulation has helped dilation. Birth must be right around the cervical corner. I keep my fingers crossed as Jackie "rubbers up." Snap! Her rubbered digits disappear between Toni's legs. I begin my sympathetic squirm as I feel the rubbered glove massage me. Vague memories of an enlarged prostate and other snapping, rubbered hands from other books. Jackie snaps the bloody glove from her hand.

"She's almost there." Almost? *Almost!* My heart begins to race. Let's get this baby born. Into diapers. Off to school. Graduated. Married. With children. There's a helluva lot more to having babies than passing out cigars.

Time for more manipulation. More snap, snap, snapping. More blood. Always more blood. And finally, Toni's recalcitrant cervix, millimeter by millimeter. . . dilates! And the sun also rises.

Sunrise. Sunday morning. August 4, 1963.

From far away in a hungover dream. Ping! Pause. Ping! Pause. Then closer, louder. Ping! My mind bolts upright. Zoom! It remembers everything. All eighteen years. Even last night with Cynthia and my friends. Too much beer. Too much music. Too much youth. Ping! I keep my eyes closed. Make my Father go away. Make it all go away. I hate myself for thinking this.

Ping! Another rock against the second-story bedroom window. I look over to where my Brother sleeps. How long before he wakes up? Never? Not even when my Father's ping is eclipsed by the soul-shattering, heart- and muscle- (the heart is a muscle) splattering ping of his hunting rifle? Did he have other dreams, other plans for this bloody Sunday? Or does he know, even now, eyes closed, asthmatic lungs struggling for air, even as he has always struggled for room to breathe in the domineering presence of our Father, does he know that if I don't go fishing, he goes hunting?

Ping! I bolt out of bed, lunge into my clothes, scramble downstairs, out the back door and into the backyard to greet my Father. Rendezvous with rage. But rage, and all of "that," is where it has always been. Smoldering. Capped and smoldering like the dormant familial volcano that it is. All hissing gasses and molten lava. The tragic eruption yet to come.

Into the backyard of my childhood, where we jumped on the trampoline, played catch with the baseball, the football, our emotions; cleaned the day's catch of trout; washed the mud from our Willy's Jeep; polished my Dad's 1955 Jaguar XK140 Roadster; built snowmen, snow castles. Capped and recapped the smoldering family volcano and stemmed the lava flow as we let the moments go and the decades pass.

Why do I know that this is different? That I am not going to fulfill the fishing dreams of my Father? That I am not going to satisfy my Mother's dreams of money for college by stacking hay with Poncho Musgrove? How do I know? I know because I am the weak one. The deadly tug of war between my parents, both of whom I love madly, has at long last become too much. I know I can no longer be two people. I fear I can no longer be one.

"It's good to see you, Dad." Lies, lies, lies. . . .

"I wasn't out late. I just forgot we were supposed to go fishing today." Lies, lies, lies.

"Gee, I thought I told you . . . I promised to stack bales today. I need the money so I can go to college." Lies. Lies. Lies.

And my Father knows. My words belong not to me but to my Mother, his estranged wife. And the lava flows. My Father steams and the hissing gasses of his soul's despair become streams of words.

Words. Always his most powerful weapon. He is, after all, a lawyer. He hates the practice of law but loves language and the power of words. The pinging pebbles against the bedroom window were meant then and always for me. I am his revenge against the world, his one chance at immortality. All else is lost. His daughter, his first-born son, lost. Tucked snugly into their Mother's nest, the nest of all sane, rational people. My Father knows that I am all he has. I am not all that I could be, but he has read me to sleep with Ambrose Bierce and H.L. Mencken, taught me the piano and the joy of duets, shared his poetry, philosophy, his wild dreams of a different life, that I might benefit from the best of him, the worst of him, and go beyond. Live what is beyond his living. For I am all he has, his last chance, and he reaches out with the molten power of his magmatic flow of words.

"How much money are you going to make stacking hay?"

"Fifteen dollars."

My Father pulls his wallet from his pocket and hands me the last three hundred dollars he has to his name.

"There. Now let's go fishing."

But we both know that it isn't about money. It is about love and devotion and the torn realization of self. The volcano rumbles. Does my Mother know she lies sleeping in the belly of the monster? Does she know my Father, her dangerously estranged husband, is about to bring the moment to its crisis, while my Brother sleeps, cocked and ready to do what can't be helped?

My Father and I are face to face. Toe to toe. Soul to soul. The three pictures of Benjamin Franklin hang in the air between us. Words fail. But he lets them flow anyway, like a puncher out on the ropes, fighting by sheer instinct. He lets them go.

"Dirk, money has no value. None whatsoever. Never put it above the living of your life. If you don't stack hay today, don't make fifteen dollars, I promise you, you will still go to college. And if you don't . . . so much the better. College isn't the answer *to anything. It is only important as an experience. So instead of college, maybe you'll hitchike through Europe or hop a steamer to some foreign country, and that will be the experience through which you will discover your life. But money has nothing to do with it. Never use it as a reason or an excuse for anything. Ever. Now. Let's go fishing."*

His final soliloquy. Of fishing and money and the stacking of hay. And we both know it has nothing to do with any of that. But he is out on the ropes. He waits for me to speak. But words have long ago failed for me. I cannot speak. Or move. My Father waits . . .

And I let him.

The wordless moment lasts for an eternity.

The lava flows, the volcano rumbles, and I erupt, for I am the weak one. The primeval scream I hear is mine and I do what I have never done. I let go. The white walls of the garage, where there used to be the Jaguar XK 140 Roadster, turn red with blood. Mine. I feel nothing. I hear only my own distant scream of rage as I beat my fists, and the volcano, dormant for eighteen years, erupts. Somewhere in the midst of my manic pounding I sense my Father near me. I turn. Our eyes lock. And the torch passes. Without saying a word, my Father speaks to me:

If you understand nothing else, understand this that I am about to do.

And nothing is said, but I know it is finished. The volcanic violence of family fury has been let loose. Nothing will ever be the same.

My Father goes to the back door of the house. I hear the shattering of glass.

The sun is up. Jackie tells me that, lo and behold, my wife's cervix is now a perfect ten! Ten big, beautiful, fully dilated centimeters! Hurray! Celebration. Plenty of room for the baby to pass through. We're nearly there. Yahoo! My spirits rise with the sun. Toni is ready for the final push. All that remains is to get our child to descend and rotate its little head into the proper position.

Jackie's friend, birthing attendant number three, arrives. Her name is Beth.

"Maybe this baby just doesn't like you," she says with a smile. I like her immediately. She has a sense of humor. And she doesn't ask for anything to eat!

Time for the Big Push. "We" push. And we push. And we push! Minutes become hours. The Big Push becomes a Big Fiasco. An exercise in futility. Jackie tries everything in her bag of tricks. Nothing works. Never in all of the hundreds of home births she has done has Jackie been so stymied. My early-morning exuberance fades as the clock moves closer to noon. The rain falling outside no longer seems romantic but only further dampens my spirits.

Jackie suggests another walk. Maybe it will help the baby's head to descend. Can Toni handle it? She nods that she is game to try. Thirty-four hours of labor and she is still positive, fearless, full of energy. I couldn't do this without her. Wait a minute, isn't it supposed to be the other way around? My God, I've got the cart before the horse. The baby before the birth. The husband before the wife. I've got it all backward. I collect myself. If Toni can walk in the rain, so can I.

As we don rain gear in preparation for the great outdoors, Jackie and Beth begin to swap tales of Kung Fu and daring do. Her, too? A student of martial arts? But then they are friends. And this is Los Angeles, where karate schools proliferate faster than shopping malls. Where having a powerful karate kick is almost as good as having a powerful lawyer, an expert plastic surgeon, your own talk show. Their conversation waxes gossipy. Beth is dying to know.

"Was he there? Tell me, tell me, tell me . . . was Chuck there? Did you meet him? Is he cute? How tall is he? Who else was there?" And more important, who wasn't there? Who got their karate ego Kung Fu'd by being left out?

I wait for Toni's contraction to pass before helping her into her rain slicker. The girls giggle and gossip as my moaning, gasping wife and I slip quietly out into the rain, leaving Beth and Jackie deep in their gossipy confab.

Does their banter reflect a wealth of confidence and calm? Or a lack of concentration and care? How can they gossip over such mundane matters while Toni and I struggle to have our first child? Maybe I'm being too sensitive? On the other hand, I am the husband, so excuse me, for crying out loud. Wasn't I supposed to merely coo into my wife's ear while midwives and birthing attendants and momma did all the real work? There is definitely more to this than passing out cigars. Maybe it should be required by law that all parents have at least one of their children by natural childbirth so that the father can know why there is and has always been a sanctity to motherhood that goes far beyond female liberation or women's rights. So men can know why, when the door opens, the food is served, or the ship sinks, it is always "women and children first." Why women deserve more respect than we can possibly ever give them. So that men can know what the pages of *Playboy* never told them. And never will.

Toni and I are outside. It is still raining. We walk down the country road in front of our house to the mailbox. Every twenty or thirty steps, Toni squats and moans and leans back while hanging onto my hands for support. It takes us an hour to squat and moan the half mile to the mailbox and back. I try not to see it as some kind of omen that the only mail for us was junk. Isn't it always? Junk mail, junk bonds, junk food. America is having a party, a veritable junket of junk.

Toni and I don't realize that all our neighbors watched our laborious squat and walk "mail run." The word is out. The Benedicts are having their baby. At home! What the neighbors don't know is that we are *trying* to have our baby at home. What they don't know, as the saying goes, can't hurt them. Can what we don't know hurt us?

We think our rainy walk is the final episode in our little drama of birth. We think our child will soon be in our arms. Our ignorance is our bliss.

Chapter Thirteen

We make our way back to the house. As we enter, I toss junk mail while Toni sheds clothes and heads for her chamber of (horrors) contractions.

Don't ever tell me that women don't love to talk about men. Because Beth and Jackie, single women in their late thirties, liberated, self-sufficient (well muscled!), are still in full swing. Nonstop chatter about the guys at the party, how they were dressed, how sexy or sexless they were, and wouldn't they just love to . . . ! I try to change the topic of conversation. To something like, say, having babies? No luck. Their rapping, hard-core, black-belt banter is really ripping.

"You should have seen the muscles in his ass!" says Jackie. "He was so cute in his black tux and red Reeboks!"

Chuck? In red Reeboks? Can't be. In the midst of all of this (and my speechless dismay), Jackie examines Toni. There is a pause in the banter. Finally we are back from the land of Reeboks and buttocks and black-belt banquets. Jackie looks puzzled.

"Yes?" I ask, unable to stand the silence any longer.

"No change," says Jackie, not looking at me.

Nooooo! It can't be. It is nearly 1:00 Sunday afternoon. Thirty-seven hours of labor!

"You mean to tell me the little bastard . . ." I catch myself. We don't know if it's a boy or a girl, if it's blonde or brunette, we don't even know if it's healthy and whole. But there is one thing we do know . . . it isn't a bastard. (Although having bastards is very chic these days in certain segments of American society.)

Jackie "snaps" to! On go the gloves. Snap, snap, snap. I hold my ears as she manipulates the baby's head in an effort to get it to turn. It doesn't.

Jackie has a plan. I don't care what it is, I'm all for it. Her plan calls for three people, six hands, and one very pregnant woman. I do a quick check. I'm ecstatic. We have all the necessary ingredients.

Here's the plan: Toni, who is wearing what has become her uniform—nothing—and I will stand facing each other. Beth will kneel behind Toni on the floor. Jackie, both hands rubbered and ready, will sit on the floor between Toni and me. The three of us are all eyeballs and crotches and very, very cozy.

Here's how the plan works: When Toni has a contraction, she holds my hands for balance and squats. I remain standing. Kneeling behind, Beth supports Toni's lower back with her hands to ease the terrible back pain that Toni is now having.

Jackie, as Toni contracts and squats, lies on the floor face up under Toni. She puts her hand up and in Toni, giving her a better angle and more leverage to rotate our reluctant child's head. With each contraction, Toni pushes. Pushes with every muscle in her body. Pushes time after time after time. Her entire body turns red with the effort. When the contractions start, Toni must push, push the baby down through the cervix, into the birth canal, and out into the world!

And when does the pushing end?

My Father pushed. Pushed everything to the edge. And beyond. Pushed my Mother, my Brother, my Sister; pushed the entire family forever beyond endurance or what we thought our endurance to be. Pushed himself. Into oblivion. Why? Because we were lazy? Because no matter what we did, it wasn't enough. He pushed us to understand there was more, always more. Of everything. Dismayed that we didn't see it, want it with the same burning passion that he did, he pushed even harder. He dreamed of constant change in a land of status quo. Dreamed of infinity in a finite world and pushed us, in spite of our terror, toward that dream.

Until finally, my Brother pushed back.

Ever wonder why in the movies, when it comes to birthing babies, they invariably get it all wrong? Never show the process, the segue. Only the final pushing. And why does the woman always lie on her back? I'll tell you why. Because men make movies. It wasn't always thus.

In the old days (how old depends on where you live), no woman worth her sex would have allowed any man near the birthing of a child. Bad energy. Only women. Women who let women have babies in any position they desired. (As they still do in less "civilized" cultures.) They had them standing, squatting, on all fours . . . they let their instincts dictate which position was best for facilitating birth. But this exclusive club "for women only" made men very nervous and they took control. As men are wont to do. The men of modern medicine knew better. Better to strap her down, spread-eagle, on cold tables. Better to clamp her feet in stirrups. Better to make her numb, make her immobile, make her powerless. Make her yours!

Of course, when it comes to sex in the movies, the men in control (producer/director/financier/actor/writer) let their boyish imaginations run wild when deciding which, among an infinite variety of positions, the female (actress) will find herself in as she fulfills the fantasies of the male producer/director/financier/actor/writer. Sometimes they even put her on her back. And of course, being experts in this field, they show the process. From pickup to foreplay. From entrance to orgasm! The orgasm of birth, unique unto the female of the species, makes men nervous as hell. The orgasm of sex they can't live without. They love the depiction of sex in any and all forms. Birth incapacitates them.

Men make war. Death is their specialty, be it real or celluloid. Women make babies. Life is their specialty. It is the one feat of which they are capable that men are not. If women were really interested in so-called liberation, they would stop letting men yank and cut their babies from their drugged-up, strapped-down bodies. They would take back their God-given control of "man"kind's destiny. They would ban, forever, all death-mongers from the sanctity of humanity's delivery room.

And perhaps then we could begin the birth of a kinder, more gentle world.

My Father was beyond the lines drawn by sexual definition. He was no longer simply the winner of bread, fighter of wars, leader of other men in their trek toward ever more manly achievements. He saw the finiteness of such roles and nurtured higher ambitions. He became female with his incessant pushing of his children toward a larger birth. Life is finite. Death is infinite, is infinity. The finite form that life takes in the birth of a child is doomed to remember the freedom of infinity from whence it came. We all hunger to experience that infinite freedom in this finite world.

I was born unto a Father whose memory of infinity was very strong. He pushed continually, with the force of a birthing mother, for his children to have that same memory. But alas, some of us are born with better memories than others. Can you remember your first kiss? First grade? First breath? First suck from the umbilical cord? Remember from before that and the galactic womb from whence you came? Can you remember the beginning? Can you remember infinity? My Father pushed us all constantly to do just that. It was tantalizing, intoxicating, stunning. It was paralyzing and it froze us all in the tracks of the little lives we struggled to live.

But I, the middle child and second son, believed in my infinite soul, my walks along the streams and mountaintops, that he was right. That I could remember the void that is beyond avoidance. Believed that, somehow, there was more than "this" to life. And my sense of failure, of not "getting the most out of life," grew from a tiny, intermittent echo to a constant cacophony of cosmic congruence. What was I to do? Catch the fish, score the touchdowns, stack the hay, kiss the girls and make them cry? What was I to do knowing that there was more to life than all the wonder of "this"? Who can live, get up in the morning and get through the day, with the weight of the universe on his shoulders?

The answer became obvious, my Father was mad. And his madness made the world around him uneasy and nervous. And when he refused to give up the madness of his willful ways, it made the world around him angry. Very angry. None of us can stand for very long the presence of someone continually telling us that we are not all that we can be. We must be rid of them. By hook or by crook or by high-powered hunting rifle. The only other solution was to admit that our Father was not crazy but right, and the rest of the family, the rest of the world, was wrong. But that was too much. That was impossible. And my Father kept pushing.

Toni pushes . . . and pushes . . . and pushes. Every hour or so Jackie, Beth, and I take breaks. For Toni there is no break. Until she breaks. The contractions will come when they will come and she must catch them when they do and push. It is essential to stay on top of them. They grow in strength. For the first time I see a crack in Toni's demeanor. Every now and then it is too much for her. She "misses" a contraction. It comes, she fails to catch it, to push through it, and it spins out of control. Her breath becomes spasmodic. Her body is seized by a spasm, epileptic in nature, and she is totally at its mercy.

Not in but out of control. It is painful. There is blood everywhere. Jackie is running out of rubber gloves. I am running out of . . . everything. There has been no progress.

It is nearly 4:00 Sunday afternoon. Forty hours of labor! Our birthing equipment lies piled around us, unused. Mocking us and our futile efforts. Hemostats to clamp the cord, bulb syringe for suctioning the baby, towels for a shower after delivery, baby clothes and receiving blankets, blood pressure cuff and meter, fetoscope, betadine solution, rubbing alcohol, fleet enema, bottle of vitamin E oil in lieu of episiotomy, tongs to handle sterile equipment, hot compresses in a crock pot that is on and ready, large bowl for placenta, towels, towels, and more towels. Etcetera, etcetera, etcetera. We are ready and waiting in hopes that this baby's head will turn, descend, and begin its journey down the birth canal. No such luck. It is heartbreaking. Jackie has done everything humanly possible. Toni has done that and, I suspect, more. We sit in silence like hosts of a surprise birthday party who have been stood up by the guest of honor.

I feel responsible. Toni is inside the experience. She is gone, gone, gone into that female world of giving birth. It takes everything she has to stay focused on the process. It is impossible for her to step outside and make objective decisions. What to do or not to do? The decision is mine. *I am responsible.*

I dangle the keys to my Porsche between Toni's legs.

"Come out, kid, and it's yours."

Toni smiles. Jackie asks for a moment to go into another room and collect her thoughts, concentrate, make sure there isn't something we could try that she has forgotten.

While she is gone, Toni and I continue to handle each

contraction as it comes. The contractions are very severe now and only a minute or so apart. Fifteen minutes go by. Jackie reappears.

"What do you think?" she asks me.

"What do I think? I'm the husband, remember? The sperm donor. You're the midwife. The expert. What do *you* think?"

She takes a half step backward, unusual for a Leo with a black belt. (I'm not a zodiac maniac, but you spend this much time sharing your naked wife with someone and you eventually swap signs.) She pauses.

"I think we should give it another hour and then take her to the hospital."

Am I getting the benefit of her wisdom? Or an admission of our failure? Without thinking, I answer, "No, this is it. We are going to the hospital. Now!"

Where did my decision come from? Toni and I look at each other. All the work, all the preparation, all the dreams of a home birth. . . . Hamlet speaks:

That it should come to this!

Toni goes into a contraction. Push, push, push.
Jackie coaches her. Push, push, push.
I go to the phone. Push, push, push.

"Sit up straight at the table," says my Father to my Brother. . . .
"Don't chew with your mouth open."
"Stop twitching your foot."
"Go to the basement and eat with the dog."

"Stop mumbling. Enunciate your words."
"How you speak is a reflection of who you are."
"Make something of yourself."
"Put the tools away when you are finished."
And finally . . . "Put the gun down!"
Push. Push. Push.
Stop Pushing!

Let go. Let go. Let go. If only my Father had. You can't get out of the way once the trigger has been pulled. But before, before you push, push, push all the right people at all the wrong times and in all the wrong places, you can change the circumstances that put you in the way. You can get out of the way before it's too late.

Maybe I should get out of the way?

It is a tragedy my Father is dead. He had only himself to blame.

It is a miracle I am alive. I have only my Father to thank.

In life, as in birth, knowing when to push and when to let go and get out of the way is the delicate deciding line between the tragedy and the miracle.

Maybe I should get out of the way?

Chapter Fourteen

W hen having a baby at home, you always make arrangements for emergency backup: a hospital and a doctor you can go to if any unforeseen circumstances arise that make a home birth impossible. Unforeseen circumstances. . . .

I have seen too much to believe in the "unforeseen circumstances" that make home life impossible. They are always there. Just because we don't see them, doesn't mean they don't exist.

There may have been those at my parents' wedding who "foresaw" all that was to come. Foresaw the incompatibility beyond any heart-felt vows the youthful, star-crossed lovers could make to the contrary. How much of life we see coming is a matter of extreme consequence.

My Father should have seen the bullet coming the second

he saw my Brother standing at the foot of the stairs. Seen it coming the minute he left me stranded in the backyard. The day he divorced my Mother. The year my Brother graduated glumly from the halls of a higher learning he never aspired to. The decades the family spent in denial of mismatched parents. The eternity he came from to be born, an only child, into his solitary childhood in the Montana town of Harlem beside the tracks of the Great Northern Railway, which his railroad conductor father, my grandfather, worked on. Some-where along that line of "unforeseen" circumstances, he should have, he must have, seen it coming. I did.

I saw it coming the first time I saw my Father pick my Mother up in his arms to swing her around and saw her go limp. "Put me down, George. Put me down," she said. And I saw my Father's despair behind the smile he gave the prying eyes and hearts of his children. What was I? Five? Six? It made me old. Yes, I saw it coming. All of it: their divorce, the family's emotional death, his death, the fear and anxiety of my own life, and the woman who would marry me in spite of all I'd seen. And pay the price.

And is this home birth gone awry part of that price? Picking up the tab for my need to push the envelope, fulfill my Father's dream of infinity, of freedom? I suspect it is.

I dial the Glendale Hospital to ask for our ace in the hole, our spiritual copout, our karmic safety net, our emergency backup . . . our Dr. Wu.

"What do you mean Dr. Wu is out of town?"

"I mean he ith out of town. He ith not available."

I try not to let the lisp bother me.

"Listen. This is an emergency. A home birth. Dr. Wu is our backup." I pause. Evidently the Lisp at the other end of the line is not getting the message. "He knew this baby was due any day. He must have left a number where he can be reached."

"I'm thorry, he ith unavailable." I begin to suspect, somehow, that the lisp is the problem. I consider putting one on so that we can begin speaking the same language.

"Well, is there thomeone . . . someone else, another doctor that I could talk to?"

A big sigh comes from the earpiece of my phone.

"Hold on a minute."

I immediately punch my ever-present stopwatch. Tick, tick, tick, tick . . . fifty-eight of them. An eternity.

"What did you thay your name wath?" asks the Lisp.

Maybe I'm getting somewhere. Maybe he'll be an "A-Team" fan. . . . Fantasy:

"Dirk Benedict! Why didn't you thay tho? We'll thend an ambulance. Don't worry about a thing. Loved your show. Whath Mithter T really like?"

"Mr. T is fabulous. Came to my wedding, as a matter of fact. Yes, the gold's real, and if you don't take good care of my wife and baby, he will come to that goddamned hospital and personally break every bone in your body. You'll never lisp again!"

"I'm thorry. There ith no Doctor who can handle your thituation," says the Lisp. And my fantasy ends.

You're only famous when you don't want to be.

"I don't think you understand. This is an emergency."

I sense I'm not going to get anywhere with this guy. Better

find out his name before he hangs up on me. You know, for documentation in case this really gets ugly.

"With whom am I speaking?"

"It doethn't matter," he glibly lisps.

"It matters to me," quoth I.

"I'm thorry," sayeth he. Must want to hang on to his anonymity. Smart guy. Wish I had.

All I wanted to do was act. I didn't know there was a catch.

"We'll let you act, if you let us make you famous."

"But I don't want to be famous. I just want to act."

"No, no, no. You don't get it. See, we won't hire you to act unless you're famous and you can't get famous unless we hire you."

"Well, let me ask you this . . . if you let me act, and I let you make me famous . . . do I have to be rich?"

"Maybe you should consider another line of work."

I want to have it both ways. To be rich and not to be rich, to have fame and not to have fame, to live and not to live, to be true to my Father and not to lose my family. . . .

Jackie, who has been with Toni, notices my mind has wandered. She takes the phone. I notice, for the first time, the size of her forearms. How could I have missed them? Great for karate chops to the neck, I imagine. The muscularity of her arms gives me confidence that she will succeed where I have failed.

Have I failed? I glance down at my own slim arms. I remember what they used to look like in my beef-eating, football-playing, Father-hugging days.

"Hello. My name is Jackie Sorenson. I'm the midwife. Dr. Wu is my backup doctor. If he has left town he had to leave a doctor to cover his patients. I would like that doctor's name."

Now we're getting somewhere!

"You mean to tell me no one is covering for Dr. Wu?"

Or are we?

Jackie tries to get a phone number, any phone number, at which Dr. Wu can be reached. The anonymous impediment on the other end of the line refuses any information. Jackie karate-chops the phone into its cradle.

Dr. Wu is gone. Or as my good friend Mr. T would say, "Dr. Wu be gone!"

> So when that baby won't be born,
> No matter what you do,
> Don't kick and scream and pound your head,
> And don't call Dr. Wu.

> Cuz' if you think you feel forlorn,
> Your wife now turning blue.
> You'll soon be wishing you were dead,
> When you call Dr. Wu.

> Yes, Dr. Wu be gone they say.
> Dr. Wu not in.
> Dr. Wu can't help you,
> And we just don't know who can.

> So woe is you, too bad for you.
> If you don't like it, you can sue.

Maybe what I really need is a good lawyer. To think I had been so pleased, in my oriental-philia, that we had a doctor of Chinese ancestry. Well, now is not the time to cry over the Occidental Oriental. Like Grandma used to say, "Occidents will happen." We have plenty of plundered civilizations littering the pages of the history of Western civilization to prove Grandma right. Maybe Dr. Wu read *Confessions of a Kamikaze Cowboy* (my "manifesto prostato") and wants to teach me a lesson. More gibberish . . .

> You say potato. I say po-tah-to.
> You say prostato. I say pro-stah-to.
> Prostato. Pro-stah-to.
> Castrato. Cas-trah-to . . .
> Let's cut the damn things off!

My mind enters the "Imaginary World of Dr. Wu." I envision the other end of our Glendale connection. Dr. Wu is not gone but stands next to the Lisp, who has me on the line.

"Who?" asks Wu.

"Dirk Benedict. He theth you're hith emergenthy backup," says the Lisp.

"Been waiting for this phone call. Tell him I took a slow boat to China," says Dr. Wu.

"I'm thorry. Dr. Wu ith out of town."

"I said slow boat to China. . . . Kick that arrogant Kamikaze Cowboy sonofabitch in those balls of his that he continually rubs in our faces. The two that got away! And now he wants us to deliver his baby?"

"If he'd lithened to hith doctor he wouldn't be in thith meth."

"That's right. No balls, no babies. Tell him I can't be reached."

"Thorry. Dr. Wu didn't thay where he could be reached."

"Let's just see what those balls of his are made of."

"Too bad. I loved that TV theries he did."

"'The A-Team'? A cartoon. Wuss show. No one ever even got shot. No blood and no balls!"

"A wuth show? Gee, Dr.Wu, I thought he . . . it . . . had real ballth."

"Get rid of him."

Didn't Dr. Wu get it? I was on his side. That is, the side of his forefathers. The side of Chinese medicine, with its Ayurvedic Indian roots and its Zen Japanese branches. Ah well, never trust an Occidental Oriental. They know too much. And anyway I'm making all this up, letting my imagination get the best of me. Maybe it is the best of me. Except . . .

Dr. Wu *is* gone and he took the Glendale Hospital with him. I assess the situation. The situation assesses me, which is what situations do: assess us, appraise us, diagnose us, evaluate us. Tell us things about ourselves that, more often than not, we don't want to know. Or remember. . . .

Chapter Fifteen

N ow that's the way to run the goddamned football!" The coach yanked me from the ground and slapped the side of my helmet. "That's the fullback we've been hearing about."

I gritted my teeth, turned from the coach, and trotted back to the huddle, hiding the few puny tears that eked out and screwed my mind to the task of shoring up the reservoir of emotion that threatened to break and sweep me and the coaches, the players, the entire football field away in a wash of clear saline fluid. I was not about to cry. Not now. I didn't cry at his death, at his funeral, or at any time in the two weeks since, and I was not about to cry now. Maybe tomorrow. Maybe next year. Maybe never?

My selection to the East-West Shrine Football Game of 1963 had made my Father very proud. It proved that you *can win without making winning your goal, succeed without worshipping success.*

After the game, he and I had planned to drive the 100 miles from Great Falls, where the game was to be held, back to White Sulphur Springs together. Give us a chance to be together, celebrate, discuss all the special moments of the game, all the touchdowns I had scored, and always how the game and touchdowns were not what the experience was really about. The game was only a few days before I would take my first big step into the world as I went off to Whitman College, where I would continue to play football, study music, and explore other facets of myself.

My Dad never made it to the game. I went for both of us. Against the advice of everyone who felt it didn't look "right" (so soon after), who felt I was going just to please (yes, even in death) my Father, felt I was not capable of playing. They weren't completely wrong.

I wasn't capable. But my heart was in the right place and my life was on the line. If I didn't go, I knew I would never go anywhere, never do anything again. I had to go through the motions. It was impossible to go through the emotions.

There was much dismay among the coaching staff, which was from Montana State College in Bozeman, at my poor performance during the practice week prior to the game. I was a much-heralded fullback with a unique if not overpowering running style. I once saw an opposing team's scouting report on me: "Great balance. Almost impossible to knock him off his feet. Need to gang-tackle." Is that what I needed? To be knocked unconscious, knocked into my subconscious?

To have the wind, the life, knocked out of me? To be knocked so flat it would take a lifetime to get up? The coaches had read the scouting reports. They should have read the "Great Falls Tribune" or "Billings Gazette" or "Helena Independent Record." Then they would have known why I was a mere shell of my former, perfectly balanced Self. I had indeed, been gang-tackled.

The harder I tried, the more I floundered, fumbled, tripped, hit the wrong holes . . . in total disgrace. My teammates figured somebody had paid somebody off. Our school was so small that I had never competed against any of them, nor had any of them seen me play. They had only heard of me. They were all big-city boys from places like Billings, Helena, Havre, Lewistown, Bozeman, Livingston. . . . I was just a small-town lad with a lot of ink, who was proving you can't believe what you read in the papers. I had also just buried the Father my Brother had shot and had testified at a coroner's inquest, but this was football and they either didn't know or didn't care. Or both. And rightly so. It wasn't their cross to bear. If you can't stand the heat, stay out of the kitchen.

If you can't stand the family, stay out in the cold. If you can't stand the blood, stay out of the bedroom. If you can't stand and be counted, don't sit quietly in judgment.

My tortured ass was taking the spot of some deserving athlete without emotional problems. Emotional problems? Me? Emotion's no problem for me. I've got emotion to burn, to lend, to drown in. But not to show. My problem is simple. I have a dead Father. Although I can't tell them that. If they don't know, they must never know. It is my deadly little secret. It makes me different. Too different.

But I did make that one glorious run during the week of practice when I broke two or three tackles, ran twenty yards, and the coaches all looked at each other and thought, "All right! Finally. He's back!"

"Now that's the way to run the goddamned football! That's the fullback we've been hearing about!"

But I wasn't. I never ran that way again. Not in practice. Not in the game on that Saturday night when the stands were full of more people than I had ever seen in one place at one time. Not once during my four-year collegiate career. Not in this lifetime. The style with which I ran was as dead and gone as the pain of my Father and the innocence of youth. The only running I would do was not towards the goal line, but away. Not towards emotion, but away. Not towards the family, but away. Not towards love, but away. Not towards life, but away. Not towards fatherhood, but away.

The pain was so great that warm August evening, when the stands were full and the noise was loud, that it made my embarrassment incidental. Much of my home-town had come to see me play, the first time one of "theirs" had been so honored. The game was close, but still the coaches, out of kindness, put me in during the second half for one series of downs. And I tried. God, how I tried to rise above death and despair and show them all that my Father had not died in vain. That life, mine included, could go on. I wanted to play with a panache and vitality that would, if not bring him back to life, at least bring back the memory of life. I tried harder than I have ever tried to do anything. Or have ever tried to do anything since. And if I broke a tackle, it was for him; if

I made a first down, it was for him; if I scored a touchdown, it was for him. But I failed. It was only going through the motions and all for nothing. And it was for him.

No Hollywood ending to this grid-ironic soap opera. No high school football hero, with the ghost of his Father cheering on the sidelines, breaking tackles, scoring the winning touchdown. What was to be the crowning achievement of my high school athletic career became instead an agonizing game I wanted only to end. The game ended. The agony went on and on and on. . . .

It took the coaching staff at Whitman College a year to realize what I already knew (but couldn't tell them). I was a mere shadow of my former slashing, dashing, well-balanced, fullback self. I wasn't the fullback of their dreams, of their scouting reports. My sophomore year, they switched me to defense. It was a match made in heaven. Someone who has been gang-tackled by life, had the life knocked out of him, knows how it is done. I shook off blocks and made tackles with the ferocity of one fighting for his life. Let someone else get the glory, make the flashy runs, the quick decisions, attract all the attention. I didn't deserve any of that. Was not capable of it. I would wait on the other side and provide grist for their glory mill. Anonymity in the trenches was a haven for the ignominy in my mind. I was safe from people who might discover my terrible secret.

My gridiron career ended not with a bang, as my Father's life had, but with a whimper.

My senior year in college, I was knocked unconscious during a game early in the season with Willamette College in Salem, Oregon. When I regained consciousness five minutes later, I could remember nothing of what happened and recognized no one.

It was bliss. For the first time since my Father's death, I was free of his ghost. With the loss of my memory, I was free of his. But alas, within the hour, my memory came back, and with it came the ghost. And I realized that what I really wanted was to forget. I wanted oblivion. Is that why I drank too much, too often? Is that why sobering up was such psychic agony?

"Heaven and earth, must I remember?" whispers Hamlet in my ear.

The week after the Willamette game, during practice, I was knocked unconscious again. This time it would not be minutes, but hours before I came to. When I awoke, I found myself once again in that familiar, blissful state beyond memory where ghosts do not dwell. I remembered nothing from before the injury, recognized nothing. No past to haunt me. No future to taunt me. Only this glorious present, lying in a hospital bed with birds singing outside in the sunshine beyond the worried fluorescent faces hovering inside. I had never been so . . . what is the word? Serene? Calm? Happy? Free! I was free. Free from the anxiety and turmoil, from the ghosts of my family's past and the terrible burden of keeping the secret.

I knew only my name. Dirk Niewoehner. And I liked how little I knew, liked where I was, how I was feeling. I *couldn't figure why everybody seemed so worried. If they only knew that this was Heaven. Is this Heaven? If so, if this is being dead . . . let me be.*

The concerned crowd parts and the most beautiful girl in the world appears before me. I want so much to comfort her. Tell her not to cry. If I am dead, if this is me lying in my coffin, as it was my Father lying in his, and she is crying for me as I yearned to cry for him, then stop. Don't cry for me, cry for the living. Cry for those who are doomed to remember. They call her Bambi. Bambi Joy. (This must be Heaven for only an angel can have a name like that.) They say she is my fiancée. She says she loves me. She kisses me. Heaven. I don't know who she is, but I love her, too. Immediately. Bambi Joy, the girl in my dream. I love her, everyone, and everything, and I never want to come back from wherever it is I have gone.

But I do. The sun goes down, the birds stop singing, and the concerned looks leave the fluorescent faces of those who hover. I come back. And I remember. Bambi's tears of sadness become tears of joy, Bambi's joy, and I remember. We are madly, traumatically engaged to be husband and wife (father and mother?), and she alone knows my terrible little secret. She alone knows the extent to which it has rendered me impotent, and it is she who has nurtured me, in loving faith of my potent potential. A faith that goes far beyond my own. And she has paid the price.

I am not an easy person to love and I am back. My memory is back. The ghosts are back. The fear is back. And the bliss is gone. Not with a bang, but a whisper. Not with a cry or with tears, but with the dry-eyed pain of one who knows too much and has said too little.

The doctors are glad I am back. The coaches are glad I am back. Bambi Lynn Joy is glad I am back. (She won't be.) I pretend to be glad I am back. But I have tasted Heaven on Earth and know it can be mine. I have tasted Heaven and know that memory is Hell. I have tasted Heaven and know that it, and it alone, is unforgettable.

And Hamlet yet again whispers in my ear, "Heaven and earth, must I remember?"

It's 5:00 Sunday evening, February 28, 1988, Agua Dulce, California. My wife has been in labor since midnight Friday. Forty-one hours of labor. We've had one birthing attendant desert us for Disneyland; another show up after her grandma's birthday party, only to eat and sleep; our midwife has squeezed us into her social life; our unborn child is being difficult; we're fifty miles from Los Angeles; and Doctor Wu has taken a powder on us. And still no baby. Things are not exactly going as planned.

The thought keeps rolling around in my brain that somebody's trying to teach me something. Twenty years of thumbing my nose at the American Medical Association and when I finally need their assistance they want nothing to do with me. I don't even know any doctors. Yes sir, somebody's trying to tell me something. Cancer, arthritis, acne, hair loss, insomnia, headaches, weight problems . . . I've survived all of them sans modern medicine, in spite of modern medicine. But now, baby, do I need a doctor! Wait a minute. That's it! Baby needs a doctor. I don't need a doctor. Toni and her umbilically connected child, they need one. Have I pushed them into something they weren't ready for?

My Father pushed us into a life we weren't ready for, imposed his will, his life's philosophy on us. He insisted we see the world through his eyes.

I was ready for a home birth, but was Toni, was the child of our dreams?

Is that why this child refuses to come into this world? It knows what father waits for him. Waits, haunted by the ghost of his Father. Is my unborn child wary of the spiritual legacy it is about to inherit? Does it wait for me to be rid of my Father's ghost before it will come, karmically unencumbered, into my arms? Must I finally say good-bye to my Father before I can say hello to my child? Cry tears of sorrow before I can cry tears of joy?

I am paralyzed. Jackie has run out of ideas. Toni, speaking between the minute-and-a-half contractions she has been pushing through all this time, mentions a doctor who delivered the baby of her friend Deborah. Deborah spoke very highly of him. When Jackie hears his name, Dr. Lane, she realizes she knows him, also. In fact, she has used him several times as backup. We decide to call him. I let Jackie do the honors. She knows him. We get his home number from Deborah.

He answers the phone. Maybe our luck is changing?

I can hear only one side of the conversation, but it is one side too many.

"He wants to know if you have insurance," Jackie tells me, cupping the phone to her shoulder.

"Yes," I say through grinding teeth. "I have insurance."

"He has insurance," Jackie dutifully reports back to the doctor. Back and forth they go as Beth and I coach Toni, whose fate, and the fate of her child, hangs in the balance. The doctor wants to know Toni's condition. He can't believe it has been over forty hours of labor and she is still strong, let alone conscious! He wants to know what happened to our regular backup doctor.

"Tell him it's a long story and there isn't time," I say. (Someday I'll write the screenplay and he can see it at his favorite cinema.)

I don't have to have the phone to my ear to know he isn't thrilled by this phone call . . . doesn't want to get involved. He smells a malpractice rat and doesn't want it to get fat on his cheese.

"What is your net worth?" Jackie asks me.

"My what?"

"He wants to know how much cash you have in the bank."

I am stunned. The world turns on credit cards, plastic is the money that feeds the flames of the compulsive consumption that greases our national slide into bankruptcy, and he wants to know how much cash I have? The country is in debt up to its ass and the asses of endless future generations, the health-care system is a fraud, I'm in (what I begin to suspect more and more) is a life-and-death situation, and this guy wants to know if I'm solvent enough to bring another little debtor into this insolvent world? Twenty years of living a life devoid of the brutal presence of America's medical practice have left me out of practice. At least they let you know what their priorities are . . . as if we could possibly forget! Money talks or doctors walk. I want to vomit. Instead, I count to ten. In Japanese.

"A million dollars! Tell him I've got a million goddamned dollars in the bank!" Jackie gives me a funny look.

"Money is no problem," she says, taking forty-two hours of stress out of my answer. The businessman on the other end of the phone is talking.

"I understand," says Jackie. "I understand. Sure. No, I wouldn't want to put you in that position."

"I want to put him in that position, whatever position that is. I need a doctor and I don't give a shit about their hospital rules and regulations!"

She doesn't pass along my message.

"Let me talk to him," I say as I reach for the phone.

Jackie sees my anger and, before I can get my hands on the phone, she hangs up. Is she protecting me? Or him?

"Dr. Lane said he'd call the emergency room and tell them we might be coming. But he won't be there and can't guarantee anything," she says.

He's no dummy. He wants nothing to do with a woman, who isn't his patient, who has been in labor for forty-two hours.

Jackie suggests that we go to the hospital in Palmdale or maybe even the Glendale hospital, where Dr. Wu used to live, and take our chances.

Forty-two hours! Where does the energy come from? For Toni, it comes from the Universe and its eternal need to recreate itself. I am driven by the demonic dreams of my past and angelic visions of my future.

Where do the birth of this child and the death of my Father begin and end and intermingle? Is this the time to push? Or to let go? The time to face my Father's ghost? Or suffer in secrecy? To push or not to push. . . .

> *To be or not to be, that is the question.*
> *Whether 'tis nobler in the mind to suffer*
> *The slings and arrows of outrageous fortune,*
> *Or to take arms against a sea of troubles,*
> *And by opposing end them . . .*

"What do you want want to do?" asks Jackie.

"Take arms against a sea of troubles, and by opposing end them."

"What?"

"Never mind. Didn't you hear the doctor? 'How much cash do you have in the bank?' This is America. Money buys justice and it sure as hell buys all the wizardry that modern medicine has in its arsenal. The best wizards go where the money is and that's where we're going . . . to the big, rich Temple of Doom in the suburbs of Beverly Hills."

We are going where the rich people go, where all the celebrities go to die from their carcinogenic lifestyles. This isn't a terminal illness, my area of specialty. We don't want their chemotherapy, their radiation, their painkillers. We want their gadgets! And that's what they are good at. This is, after all, America.

I tell Toni we are going to the hospital. She tells me she loves me. I kiss her, assure her everything will be all right. Jackie isn't thrilled. Should I kiss her and tell her everything will be all right?

"It's fifty miles to Cedars Sinai," she says.

"Is this baby going to be born in the next hour?" I ask.

"No."

"Have we tried everything possible?"

"Yes."

"Then I'm taking Toni to Cedars!"

I think my Father waits for me there.

I start packing a bag for Toni. Beth continues to coach Toni through her contractions, which, of course, have continued through all of this. I am awed by her endurance and good spirits, by her lack of fear.

I'm afraid my Father waits for me there. Waits for me to say good-bye. Waits for me to cry.

Food. I must take food. One thing I know is that the food in hospitals is not meant to be eaten. If their cutting and their chemicals and their radiation don't get you, their food will! They can cook it, serve it, and God knows you will pay for it, but there's no law that says you have to eat it. (Natural law says you shouldn't.)

Iatrogenicide. Patricide. Suicide. (Natural law says you shouldn't.) I've known them all. I speak from experience. From both sides of the bedpan. From both ends of the barrel. From Father to Son. . . .

Toni is dressed. The food is packed. The clothes, for Toni and the baby after it is born, are packed. I turn to Toni. Time to go. I am consumed with love for her. What she has endured, the character she has shown, the courage! She embodies everything I dream of being, and know I don't deserve.

We always deserve what we get.

How did she find me? Why did she choose me? She knows of my demons, that I hear voices. I have told her everything. I tell her everything is going to be (or not to be) all right.

> *And what so poor a man as Hamlet is*
> *May do to express his love and friending to you,*
> *God willing, shall not lack. Let us go together,*
> *And still your fingers on your lips, I pray.*
> *The time is out of joint. Oh, cursed spite,*
> *That ever I was born to set it right!*

Chapter Sixteen

We inch our way downstairs and out into the early evening rain. I help Toni into the passenger side (the suicide seat?) of my Porsche 911. The car that Starbuck bought. Jackie gets in the car with the shiny tires. She is going to follow us to the hospital. I tell her I will be driving very fast, that I am not waiting, and she will be on her own to get there as soon as she can. She doesn't like being left behind like this, but she already is as I slam the door and head down the driveway. I glance at the clock in the car, it is 6:30 p.m. Forty-two and one-half hours, and still counting. Time waits for no man. No, nor baby, either. The Porsche's engine purrs. God bless German engineering. The perfect car for the situation. I take a deep breath, grab another gear. This is it. Away we go. High speed on the highway.

My Father always admired beauty. Maybe that was the elixir that hid my parent's incompatibility. Because my Mother was (is) beautiful. I saw the wedding pictures: raven black hair, green eyes, porcelain skin. A figure that curved in all the right directions and in all the right places. A beauty to take your breath and steal your heart away. God showing off. I have seen pictures of the great screen beauties. Met a few. My Mother was all of that and then some. Ingrid Bergman and Elizabeth Taylor rolled into one Montana farm girl of Swiss/German ancestry.

Yes, my Father admired beauty, married beauty, and in 1953 he bought beauty: an MG sports car. Sherwood green with a roll-down top. It was the talk of the county. Then, in 1955, as the fruits of his Robin Hood law practice began to pay financial rewards commenserate with the moral, he traded his beautiful MG for a thing of even greater beauty: a brand-new, white Jaguar XK140 Roadster with red leather interior. It was the talk of the state. People drove for miles just to catch a glimpse of it. They came in from their ranches to see this vision of elegance and speed as it passed through the wide spot in the road where they came once a week to gather their mail. Came to see it as my Father gassed it up on his way to find some sheepherder, visit an Indian reservation, have lunch with the governor, or irritate the hell out of the Supreme Court in Helena. It might as well have been a spacecraft from outer space as a sports car shipped from England.

It broke my little Sister's heart. She was eight and had considered the MG part of the family. To me, the Jaguar was romance and magic and adventure. I learned that how we get where we're going is more important than the getting there. It would be the car in which I would learn how to drive. How to double-clutch. How to do a four-wheel drift around the dirt roads of rural (was there any other kind?) Montana. The car in which I would begin to learn how and why to admire beauty, not for its own sake but for the effort and care that went into its creation.

In the dead of winter, with the top down and wearing his Eddie Bauer down-filled parka, Dad would pull my Sister and me on sleds tied to his gleaming white spacecraft with thirty-foot lariat ropes. One of the few times in Montana a lariat had anything other than a calf at the end of it. And away we would go, my Sister and I tied to our Father's glistening chariot with the crystalline blue sky above us and the winding, white country road below. Mother Nature was our Disneyland and this was our Matterhorn, our ride to end all rides. The roller coaster of our dreams.

I never stopped to consider what pleasure it may have given my Father. Was the joyride he gave the joyride he got? Sliding, spinning, laughing, grinning, tumbling through the cold air and warm glow of our childhood with our Father shifting gears, double-clutching, four-wheel drifting through the frigid air and despair of his unfulfilled dreams. Pulled by the power and grace, the love and eccentricity of a man gone mad with his need for thrill and adventure. And love.

A forty-five-year-old man in his glimmering Jaguar Roadster races down the country lane. Thirty feet behind him at the end of their ropes (as he was at the end of his), an eight-year-old girl and her ten-year-old brother hang on for dear life, having the time of their lives.

Sleigh bells ring, are you list'nin'?
In the lane snow is glist'nin.'
A beautiful sight, we're happy tonight
Walkin' in a winter wonderland!

Oh, yes. The time of our lives. And then things heated up. The snow melted, the sleds grew rusty, the marriage unbearable. The Jaguar raced head-on into a cement wall, its driver fast asleep at the wheel (but later miraculously alive and ready to rush head-on into "accidents" more fatal), and we all grew afraid. And apart.

The Jaguar was a total loss. Sold for parts. The family too, soon after, became less than the sum of its parts.

But for those brief moments, years, there was nothing like it. Before or since. On this earth.

Later on, we'll conspire
As we dream by the fire.
To face unafraid the plans that we made . . .

I hit a pothole in the freeway. My mind comes back. Toni yelps in pain. "I'm sorry, darling." I must keep it smooth, fast but smooth. My Father taught me well how to handle a car, if not life, at high speed. Now is the time to put it to use. Toni's contractions are only two or three minutes apart, very strong, and they last for over a minute.

The small interior of the Porsche is filled with drama. A woman writhes in the final throes of childbirth as a child struggles to be born. Her husband mops sweat from his brow in unison with the windshield wipers as they wipe rain from the windshield, and he babbles words of encouragement.

"Hang on, darling. Are you all right, darling? It won't be long now . . . I love you."

Toni looks at me and smiles. We remember the many trips to Montana in this car. Just the two of us. Things have changed. Now there is a third . . . the child in her belly, its head turned at an awkward angle. And a fourth . . . the voice of my Father: admiring my driving skills, whispering in my mind. Asking to be forgiven? To be released? Is his spiritual destiny (and mine) tied to the fate of our child, as that child is tied to its mother by an umbilical cord? Kill the Father, inherit the ghost.

It isn't a Jaguar but a Porsche. It isn't Montana but California. It isn't snowy rural roads but rain-filled interstate pavement, and there are no lariat-roped sleds stretched behind, but this is the roller coaster ride to end all roller coaster rides. My Father's voice whispers. And I know the Father who has haunted me forever waits for me to become what I have feared most. All my life. A father.

"It's going to be all right, darling." I turn the windshield wipers up a notch, press the accelerator down a notch. Vvvvrrroooooooom. Down the interstate and into the rainy, black night, a rooster tail of rain in our wake.

Porsches attract highway patrol officers the way Hollywood attracts beauty contest winners. I know what is certain to happen. And I can't wait. I long to see the flashing lights in my rearview mirror. I hunger for the inevitable.

"Do you realize how fast you were going?"

"Yes, officer, I do. And I wish I could go faster. My wife is pregnant, my child is being difficult, and my Father is waiting. So give me a ticket. Give me hell. But first give me an escort to the hospital. Turn on those beautiful flashing red and blue lights that I've seen so many anxious times in my rearview mirror. Let me lasso my car to your bumper and let's get this roller coaster ride on its way."

But it is not to be. I keep searching my rearview mirror. Nothing. I can't believe it. Maybe Dr. Wu and the California Highway Patrol are in cahoots. It is Sunday evening. Thousands of people are returning to Los Angeles after a weekend of leisure away from its stress and strain. The freeway is bumper to bumper. The rain falls in torrents. Surely, somewhere in the fifty miles from our house to the hospital an officer of the many laws I am breaking will come to my rescue.

I weave in and out of the stop-and-go traffic. People swear at me, chase me, make vulgar gestures in my direction. Where is that police officer when I need him? When I can go 100 miles an hour, I go 110. When I can go 80, I go 90. Sometimes I get trapped behind slower traffic and I creep in and out of it at 60. I have owned my Porsche for ten years. I know how to get a speeding ticket, how to get a highway patrol car to appear out of thin air. I know how to troll for cops. Have I lost my touch?

I am as drenched with sweat as the car is with rain as I drive like a man possessed. Which I am. I roar down Sunset Boulevard. Remember Gloria Swanson and the wonderful woman and friend she was. Run three red lights, turn right, and head down Doheny Drive at 60 miles an hour. Accelerate to 90 to catch the green light where Doheny intersects Santa Monica Boulevard. Still nary a cop in sight. Toni moans and gasps for breath between contractions with never a word of complaint, self-pity, or fear. She has to breathe through the contractions without pushing. It is important, now, that she doesn't push for fear the baby will descend and we will have to deliver it in the front seat of my Porsche. We are animals, struggling to survive this roller coaster ride to end all roller coaster rides.

I turn left off of Doheny Drive onto Beverly Boulevard. The Rolls Royces and limousines are lined up in front of Chasens, a restaurant with rich and famous patrons, several of whom turn at the sound of my screeching as I swerve around slower, saner traffic. They shake their heads in amazement. If only they knew.

At last, the emergency-entrance sign of Cedars Sinai Hospital flashes in front of me through the rainy darkness. I do a perfect four-wheel drift (thank you, Dad) into the nearest parking space. Check the clock: 7:15 p.m.

I've made the fifty miles to the hospital in forty-five minutes. Fifteen of those miles through city traffic, and all fifty in a driving rain that has traffic stopped and slowed all over Southern California.

There doesn't seem to be anyone about. Must be a slow Sunday evening. The ambulances are probably all bogged down in the rain. (Like the highway patrol?) Not me. Not us. We made it! Now if we can just get to the doors.

I grab Toni's suitcase and run around to help her out of the car. She no sooner gets out when a contraction seizes her. She squats. When its over, we start for the automatic glass doors fifty feet away. Halfway there, another contraction starts: another squat, more animal sounds. Finally a security guard sees Toni squatting on the pavement. He has seen everything, working the emergency entrance to a major hospital. The sight of Toni moaning and groaning on the pavement doesn't phase him. Then he glances at me. That gets him. He knows an expectant father when he sees one, and he's seen a few, but his experienced eye sees more . . . someone who has seen (or is about to see) a ghost.

One look at me and he rushes out, pushing a wheelchair. Is it for me? I don't need a wheelchair. I need courage. He pushes the chair up to Toni. She laughs and climbs in. The sight of her in that wheelchair, still laughing after all this time as she is wheeled into the hospital, gives me a jolt. Gives me courage. I follow the wheelchair, follow my wife, follow my baby, follow my destiny. . . .

Chapter Seventeen

*D*uke Ellington is in town. It is the fall of 1965 and the beginning of my junior year. I've been alive twenty years, my Father's been dead for two, and I've been in love for an eternity; or two months if you're on the outside looking in, which I'm not. I have spent money I don't have for two tickets to hear Duke on his one night in Walla Walla.

His was the music of my Father's record collection and I grew up listening to him and others of his ilk and era as I dreamed of someday playing my Conn Constellation trombone in a big band like his. That dream is on hold. Others are in the making.

I sit in the open window of my off-campus apartment. The "A Train" wails through the October night air. A fire burns in the tiny fireplace. My two tickets lie on the desk next to my unopened schoolbooks. I'm not at the concert because Bambi Lynn Joy has made previous arrangements. We are early but deep into our college love affair. If I go a day without the sight, the smell, the touch of her, it is a day not worth living. Before we met and fell in love she had promised someone else that she would take the "A Train" with him. I pleaded with her to cancel. She refused, being a woman of honor. Left me and my unused tickets behind and went to hear the music of my childhood with someone other than me. I am not taking it well.

Will she laugh at his jokes? Will her eyes twinkle the way they do when they look at me? How can he not try to hold her, to kiss her? She is so beautiful, so intelligent, so . . . everything. I am obsessed with a love that I know, in my secret part, I don't deserve, and it feeds the fires of fantastic jealousy. I am jealous of the very air she breathes, that it can know her, be inside her, in a way I have yet to be. This is my first leap into the lunacy of love. My heart aches. I am in a state of misery just this side of suicide.

I sit in the window, cool air in front, fire behind, and listen to the Duke. How long before I must tell her?

My Father's ghost has followed me to college, followed me everywhere. But I keep him hidden. As far as my college friends know, my Father is not a ghost but alive and well and practicing law in Montana. They can't wait to meet him, he sounds like such a terrific guy. It is my terrific secret and I planned to keep it forever, but then I met Bambi Lynn Joy and love has no secrets.

I want, need, to tell her everything, bare my soul, hold nothing back. She doesn't know why there is so much pain in *the love I give or why it was so slow to come when hers was there at first sight. At first insight. But she knows there is "something." I deny it, for fear that it will reveal too much. The feelings she has aroused in me come from the same place as those I held for my Father. My ability to express my love for her is frozen in time, in that time on August 4, 1963.*

It has been two months since we first met, and with each day, as our love grows beyond reason, it becomes ever more difficult to keep my deadly secret. If she ever knows the truth, she will know what I know: that I don't deserve her. Don't deserve her love.

The A Train leaves. The concert is over and the Duke is gone. The window is down, my guard is up and the fire is embers. There's a knock on the door and my heart's ache enters. She comes into my arms. Her prior arrangement is over and she is mine. It is the only time since we met that she has been with anyone besides me. We both know it will be the last. As long as we last. How long? Oh Lord, oh Lord, how long? Not long before I give her my fraternity pin . . . she slides out of her clothes; an engagement ring . . . under my skin; a wedding band . . . we are lips and tongues and surging energies of polarized love. Her body arches in the glow of the dying fire. She is mine, body and soul, for the taking. My hands find her every place. I am blind with motion, with passion and emotion. And in my blind desire, my heart hesitates and I see my Father's ghost. He watches as she pulls me out of my shirt, pulls me out of my pants, but she cannot pull me out of my Self, out of my terror at being found out. The potency of my secret renders me impotent. And my Father watches.

"What is it, Dirk?"
"Oh, Bambi. . . ."
"What? What is it?"
"I have done a terrible thing."
"What?"
"My Father."

*My father! Methinks I see my father . . . In my
mind's eye. . . .*

*Bambi pulls the blanket over our nakedness, all moist
and limp with the ghost of our passion. But nothing can
hide my impotence from me now. Nor its source. My Father's ghost is everywhere in the room. He sees everything.
Can she not see him? He permeates my every pore.*
"What about your Father?"
"He is dead."
"But you said . . ."
*"I know. But he isn't. He is dead. . . . And I think, I
mean I understand that I didn't, but I think . . . I killed him."*
*The ghost watches. But I don't care. My pain and
passion drive me, and I tell her what I have never told
anyone. I tell her what I do not tell myself. I relive, for the
first time, that moment in time on August 4, 1963. I relive
what I could not live through . . .without paying a price. I
tell her the whole story. She knows the price.*

O horrible, horrible, most horrible.

Laughing is possible. Crying is possible. Even sex is possi-

ble because it can all be faked, acted. But love is not possible. Because love is what this is all about. Love of parents, love of Brother, love of Self! And love cannot be faked or acted. Love cannot be denied.

"And I love you, Bambi."

You are not part of my past, part of my terrible secret. You are this moment, the future (my salvation?), and my desire to make love with you is impossible to fake. Or be denied. And she understands. She knows the horrible truth of me, how complete my failure, and she understands. She holds me. Forgives me my failure. My impotence. She cries. For me. I feel something move deep inside, feel something in my secret place let go, relax. A little. For the first time and just enough. My Father no longer haunts the room, reminding me of my responsibilities to him, to life, and to the living of it . . . reminding me of my failure. She raises me up. Makes the intangible tangible, the impotent potent. And out of pain, we make love. But I do not cry.

And after that, after college, after all the making of love and abortions of love and tormenting it beyond repair, I stand in a phone booth in Flint, Michigan, in 1969, two weeks before my marriage to her and I ask her, "Why?"

She says she will tell me when we're old and gray. And I do not cry. I get drunk for a day, stay sick for a week, and remain heartbroken for years, but I do not cry. Because no matter how deep the pain, how real the anguish, it pales compared to what went before, and for that I did not cry.

And after she is gone (but not my love for her) . . . the ghost comes back . . . because he never left. (Is that why she did?) I never let him.

The man behind the desk looks at Toni who is gasping and smiling in her wheelchair. He looks at me. Does he know my secret? That my Father haunts me still. That I have come such a long way to get to this moment. Come forty hours through a failed attempt at home birth; come fifty miles through the rain, without a police escort; come forty-three years through the pain, without a tear; and that is a long, long way to go. I don't know what to say, so I say what doesn't need to be said.

"My wife's about to have a baby."

He gives me a look. Yes, I can see that, but what else? I can't tell him what else. It is all too complicated and painful and I have yet to tell it to myself.

"Who's your doctor?" he asks, interrupting my Jimmy Stewart stammer.

Of course! Why else would we be here? Nobody shows up at this joint, at these prices, to audition doctors for the job of delivering their baby. He assumes we know what we're doing, whom we're seeing. I see my opening. I look him straight in the eye . . .

"Dr. Peter Lane."

He picks up the phone, dials, and asks for Dr. Lane. I spoke to him only an hour ago. I pray the good doctor lied when he said he wouldn't be here and if he is here, that he hasn't forgotten me already. This is, after all, Hollywood. I know just how short memory can be. Here today, canceled tomorrow. Remember me? I'm the guy who said he was worth a million dollars! He's a doctor, surely he will not have forgotten that. Then again this is Hollywood . . . who isn't worth a million dollars? Maybe it's better he doesn't remember.

"Dr. Lane, your patient is here," says the man behind the desk. The doctor is in! I know what's coming next.

"What is your name again?" asks the man behind the desk. He remembers me; he remembers me not? I know it is now or never. My mind reels. Wait a minute. I'm an actor, for God's sake! People pay me thousands of dollars to "re-create" reality. I didn't play Lieutenant Starbuck or Faceman for nothing. These guys could talk their way in and out of any situation. I shift gears. Magic time! Seize the moment. Get the mouth going. All of a sudden, and for the first time in hours, I know exactly what to do. Forget the past forty-three hours. It's time to create a scenario to match the demands of the moment. Just like the politicians. Dr. Lane is on the line. Now to get him on the hook! I grab the phone and seize the moment! I know that this is the most important performance of my life. If it works I'll name the baby Oscar! My mouth begins to move.

"It's me, Doc. Dirk Benedict." The good doctor groans at his bad fortune. He remembers me! Is that good? Is it bad? . . . Action!

"I'm here with my wife. Just take a look at her. Will ya, Doctor? Will you do that? I know she's been in a very long, slow-progressing labor. But she's still very strong and she's fully dilated. The baby is just in an unusual position with its head turned. But its vital signs are strong. Turn the head, Doc. Just turn the head and I know we got us a newborn. Don't say anything. Just take a look at her. Just examine her. If you see she is in trouble, if you think she can't handle it, we'll go elsewhere. I promise. I'm outta here. We'll go to Burbank, to Van Nuys, to Glendale. To the moon. We're outta your life. We never happened. Just take a look. And don't worry about money. I'm loaded. Been saving my entire life for this moment. My first child. I'm forty-three years old, Doc. You give me a baby, I'll give you everything I have. My airplane, my car, my pad in Montana. My undying respect and devotion. . . . Everything. (Even my 'A-Team' residuals.) Nothing matters but my wife and this child. Please. Just take a look at her. . . ."

I stop to catch my breath. In the pause I hear his wheels turning. This is all on instinct and happening very fast. I hold the breath I caught. Instinct holds my tongue. Seconds pass in silence. The wheels of fate turn. Toni is beside me, contracting, gasping, smiling. God I love this woman. How does she do it? The wheels stop.

My fate cries out. . . .

The doctor speaks. "I'll probably regret this for the rest of my life, but okay, I'll look at her." My heart skips a beat.

Regret this for the rest of his life? I know what it means to "regret" the rest of your life. For the rest of your life. It means discontent. It means unhappiness. It means guilt and penitence. It means pangs of conscience. It means anguish, grief, heartache, and pain. It means sickness, remorse, sorrow, and woe. It means death. I wouldn't wish it on my worst enemy . . . have I wished it on myself? Regretfully yours, Your Son.

"You fill out the admitting forms. I'll send a nurse to get Toni." I want to thank him, tell him he won't regret this, but my mind has wandered and the phone is dead. I hand it back to the man behind the desk. Move quickly before they change their minds. Before they find out who I am and what terrible things I've done. Before they look up "regret" in the dictionary.

I look for my Father's ghost. I know he is here, waiting for me. As he has always waited.

"Dr. Lane says I should fill out the forms." The person behind the desk waves his hand and another person appears out of nowhere. I'm being handed off. This is a good sign. I kiss Toni. Everything will be all right. She smiles. I tell her I love her, that I'll join her as soon as I fill out the forms. She is wheeled into an elevator. I watch her disappear behind the guillotine of closing doors. It is the first time we have been separated in nearly two days. Standing alone in the hallway, I am engulfed with premonition, foreboding, a delicate balance between dread and anticipation. Between the Father that was and the father that is to be . . . or not to be.

I am led down corridors. I feel my Father lurking. Into a small office. A round young girl behind a computer hands me forms. I give her insurance cards. She is chipper, chubby, and efficient. I want to hug her. Will my arms reach? Too much hospital food. In no time at all the forms are filled. I have no idea what I've signed. I don't care. I just want to find Toni, to be there when the doctor examines her. A nurse comes and gets me. She whisks me into an elevator, then out of the elevator, down more corridors, and into a changing room.

"Where's my wife?"

"Put these on over your clothes," says the nurse, ignoring my question. I climb into my hospital greens. Battle fatigues? Another good sign. I am now one of them. They whisk me down more corridors. Covered in green from head to toe, we pass doctors, covered in green from head to toe. I look like one of them! I'm on a team. I belong. I begin to get euphoric. I'm falling in love—with hospitals, with doctors, with nurses, with all the things I've avoided for the last twenty years of my life. I adore my wonderful, baggy, green hospital garb. Will they let me take it home when I leave with my wife and baby and . . . fatherhood? All the things I've avoided for all my life.

Lead me. Take me. I am ready. I'll follow you anywhere. The ghost of my Father beckons. The time has come. I am not afraid. Green, fearless, and euphoric, I follow . . . down endless glowing corridors of fluorescent memories.

Go on . . . I'll follow thee.

My heart cries out. Toni sits pertly on the delivery table. Warren Beatty stands in front of her, talking very quietly and calmly to her. This can't be. It is! He holds out his hand to me. My Father holds out his hand to me.

"You must be the father?"

Must I? Must I?

It isn't Warren . . . too young, too handsome . . . I take his hand. "Dirk Benedict. I can't tell you. . . ."

My Father smiles. Oh, God! My Father fills the spinning room. I am not Dirk Benedict but Dirk Niewoehner. I am not the father, but the son.

O all you host of Heaven! O earth! What else?
And shall I couple Hell? Oh, fie! Hold, hold, my
  heart,

And you, my sinews, grow not instant old
But bear me stiffly up. Remember thee!
Aye, thou poor ghost, while memory holds a seat
In this distracted globe. Remember thee!
Yea, from the table of my memory
I'll wipe away all trivial fond records,
That youth and observation copied there,
And thy commandment all alone shall live
Within the book and volume of my brain,
Unmixed with baser matter. Yes, Yes, by Heaven!

But I've had enough of the observations of youth, unmixed with the baser matter of my own life. Because it is my life on the line, my wife on the table, my child to be born. Not yours. Not yours. My life, my death. Not yours. My wife, my marriage. Not yours. I saw the failure. But it wasn't mine. *It was not my failure.* I saw the smoking rifle and heard you cry. But you cried not for me; you cried for you. For your life and the death it gave you. For what you had done. Not for what had been done to you. "We always die by our own hand," I heard you say.

And when the smoke cleared and you were dead, but not gone . . . asking me to . . . what? To fulfill your dreams? To show the world that you had not lived in vain? To absolve you of your sins? Were you not ready, caught too soon in midlife, with all your imperfections still on your head? Am I supposed to follow, too?

But I am the father of this moment. Not you. "And thy commandment all alone" cannot live in the "book and volume of my brain." No more. I stood by you, stood up for you, till the end of you. And then on, into the beginning of me. And now it is time for yet another beginning, another father, another son. And I must cut the cord. *I must cut the cord*

But he doesn't go away. He knows there is more to come. He wants to hear it all.

And so do I.

Chapter Eighteen

I'm Peter Lane."

He drops the title from his name. I like this guy. He wears his greens loosely, disheveled. Daring those germs to contaminate any of his patients. I love this guy. He has said yes. Time to keep my mouth shut.

He assures Toni he will use no drugs, that there will be no IVs. This birth will be as natural as possible. Evidently he and Toni have had a talk. He has met the force of her will. He turns down the lights. At long last, the moment of truth. Four or five people come in to assist. The troops are gathering. He shows me a good place to stand, next to Toni on her right side. Where I have always stood. Where I stood when we said we would, "till death do us part." I can hold her hand from here, be out of the way, and still see everything.

Be out of the way . . . it is so hard for me to do. To get out of the way of my own destiny. I got out of the way as the rifle swung in my direction. Got out of the way of what was out of control, out of my control. Have I spent my life in compensation? Freaked into absolute control of everything that has followed that one insanely uncontrollable moment? Regretfully, Your Son. But what could I have done?

I came through the kitchen, into the living room, turned to see the rifle leveled. "Put down the gun," you said . . . and then . . . "Put down the gun." And then there was this . . . explosion . . . this roar, within and without. I hear it now. Have listened to it all my life. My heart roars, my mind roars, my soul roars; my waking, sleeping life roars with the uncontrollable memory of getting out of the way. But what could I have done? And I heard you say, "Oh, my God . . ." and I roared into the front room. Exploded into my Self. And then, I took control.

Things are moving very fast now. The room is charged with energy. The support team has been briefed. They all know our rap sheet: a home birth gone sour, forty-three hours of labor, fifty miles to the hospital . . .

The door to the delivery room opens and another green-garbed apparition slides into our midst. I recognize the muscled arms. Jackie introduces herself to the doctor and moves expertly to the left of Toni. If I am the husband, she is the maid of honor. The doctor assures Toni once again he will keep this birth as absolutely natural as possible. He explains everything as he goes. A gadget is placed on Toni to monitor the baby's heartbeat. I am glad no such monitor is hooked to me to reveal the pounding of my heart.

For I can see the ghost. It watches me closely as I teeter on the brink of fatherhood. I can see the ghost and it is my Father. And he has come to watch. The sins of the Father fall on the son, but I do not want that for this child pushing to be born. I will not have it hear the roar that I hear. The roar of my soul's inheritance.

My heart pounds and the spirit of my Father watches. For he knows there is more to come, knows there is something of him, for him, in the child we struggle to bring forth. Blood is the glue that binds. Blood is the river of infinity on which he wishes to sail free.

Everything is in place. The doctor tells Toni that with the next contraction, she should push as hard as she can. Everything is a blur. I tell myself, "Remember this, remember all of this, this is the moment of truth, the final chapter in the story of the birth of your child. The final nail in your Father's coffin. Remember this, who you are in this moment, what you think, feel in this moment, this final moment of childlessness."

But it is all happening too fast and I am not in control. My fate is in the strength of Toni to deliver, in the technology of medicine, in the hands of strangers.

I am standing out of the way, where I can see everything but can do nothing. Powerless. My fate is in the hands of others and it cries out.

I stand roaring on the verge of fatherhood, the consummation of manhood, which I have avoided all my life. I am outside myself with anticipation to see, catch, hold the miraculous expression of Toni's and my love for each other. I must remember this. But it is all happening so fast.

And the ghost gets in the way.

Rest, rest, perturbed spirit.

But he will not. For he knows there is more to come.

Toni asks that her feet not be confined by the stirrups that are usually used. Peter agrees immediately. Instead two arms are swung into place against which she can push with her feet, unhampered. Jackie talks to Toni, coaching, advising. Peter sits directly in front. Snap! Snap! Snap! I jump. Rubber-gloved memories of the home birth we never had. Peter agrees with Jackie's diagnosis. The baby's head is stuck (which is not, of course, the way he put it, but the medical jargon escapes me); the head has not rotated into position, has yet to engage, although it is further along than it was before our lawless forty-five minutes at 100 miles an hour. All my screeching, careening, and bouncing seem to have helped. Has "Porsching" helped where pushing failed?

The door to the delivery room opens. There is another doctor in the room, a woman. She comes to the left side of Toni with a smile on her face. She has heard rumors of the drama unfolding in the delivery room down the hall.

"You guys don't have anything better to do on a rainy Sunday afternoon?" Sense of humor. "Rumor is we were your last choice." The corridors must really be buzzing.

I notice she's a little overweight.

She leans in close to Toni. "I hate you. You're a week overdue, with forty hours of labor, and you look better than I do!"

She's with child! That explains her chubbiness. This is yet another good sign: a pregnant, female doctor. Not that many women doctors, and to get one who is pregnant herself . . .

what are the odds on that? A very good sign. The more women the better, as far as I'm concerned. Surround me with women.

"Three months and I'll be where you are. Only, God knows, I won't look as good."

Peter tells Toni to give it everything she has on the next contraction. Toni pushes. Two days without sleep, forty-three hours of this, but she's still going strong. The blood vessels on her forehead and neck pop out. She turns bright red. I wonder what her blood pressure is.

I will match the power, strength, and endurance of any woman in labor with that of any muscleman in any muscle parlor anywhere. If there ever was a physical endeavor that the human body should be in shape for, this is it. Separates the real women from their flabby, out-of-shape cesarean sisters.

Jackie coaches Toni. I watch. Out of the way and speechless. Our pregnant doctor friend leans on top of Toni's abdomen with both of her arms and, as Toni pushes and Peter tries to move the baby's head with his rubbered hand, our pregnant friend pushes down with all of her fecund body weight. The force being applied is staggering. Toni is the color of a ripe tomato. And yet . . . nothing. The contraction ends.

In the pause, Toni gathers her strength, Jackie murmurs words of advice and encouragement, Peter explains what is happening. . . .

Here comes another contraction and away we go. Nothing. Try again. And again. But the baby's head doesn't budge. This goes on until I, who am doing nothing, can stand it no longer. At last Peter puts me out of my misery.

He turns to an assistant and asks for something. Time for

the gadgets that only money can buy. A strange-looking machine is wheeled into place beside him. He tells Toni he is going to try suctioning the baby out. Suck the baby from the womb the same way you suck dirt from a carpet. An appropriate, if disturbing, analogy.

A long tube with a conical end to it is slid up inside Toni and attached to the baby's head. One of Peter's assistants flips the switch and it's "Hoover time." The contraction comes. Peter pulls, Toni pushes, Dr. Momma presses. I brace myself. . . .

Thwack!

What in the hell was that?

A bolt of adrenalin goes up my spine. . . .

And I am off and running. The crowd roars. My Father is one of them. It is early May 1963, and he has taken the time (out of what little he has left) to come to Billings to watch me run in the Southern Divisional Track Meet.

Track is not my specialty, certainly not distance running. I started competing in the half mile as a fluke, something to do in the spring of my senior year. An excuse to go on the road trips with my friends as I prepare for my Father's death and the end of innocence. I have never run distance before.

I placed second in the half mile at the District Track Meet in order to qualify for this race. He was there, too. Walked with me after the race as I vomited in the agony of running on will and determination and not the benefits of proper training.

But this is different. I have trained for this. It is a month later and I have been running every day. I know I can get my time below the 2 minutes and 12 seconds it was at the district meet. I was clocked at 2:05 the week before this meet. Now, with the benefits of proper training, all it will take is will and determination. And, God knows, I have proven I have that.

Thwack!

The starter's pistol fires. I and my seven competitors are off and running. Two laps, 440 yards each. They run to win. I run for reasons much more complex.

I can feel the weight of my Father's eyes on my back. I know what is expected of me: to do my best. That is all that has ever been asked. But my best has always been too good, has always gotten me what others want. Music awards, football, basketball, scholarship awards . . . my best has always given solace to everyone but me. It hides me from the world, from my family, from him. And I need to lose. To fail. To show them . . . to show him . . . my best is the worst part of me.

The crowd roars as we finish the first lap. I run comfortably in second place. It is faster than I have ever run. I am doing better than I have ever done. We cross the starting line. One lap to go. I can feel the strength in my legs, chest, and arms. I can feel my Father's eyes, feel his joy in my excellence, in my youth and the sheer, innate, power of it. I am my future and I am his.

We round the first turn of the last lap. I am still second. The boy ahead of me is the best half miler in the state. I know it is a surprise to those who watch. I am the dark horse, the Cinderella, the football player turned track man. I didn't have a chance. My lungs begin to hurt, but my *legs and heart are strong; I feel as if I can run forever. Down the backstretch, neck and neck with the leader. He glances over at me. I see his surprise. I am in shape for this moment. The taste in my mouth is familiar, the taste of victory. I am eighteen years old, running like the wind; my life stretches out in front of me. I am going to show them. I have it all. Young and handsome and strong and talented and bright, my life stretches before me . . . and the pain within is beyond bearing. I am going to show him.*

I stand on the infield of the track gazing up at the cloudless spring sky. A hawk soars in the distance. The race finishes in a dream across the field. People run toward me from several directions. They surround me with questions.

"What happened?"

"You all right?"

"Cramps?"

"Pull a muscle? . . ."

And then my track coach: "What happened for Christ's sake? You were there. You had it won. Only 220 yards to go! Jesus, I never expected this. . . ."

Not you. But someone should have. As someone should see what is yet to come.

I look from the soaring hawk to my striding Father as he comes through the people and they drift away.

"It's all right, son. It's all right."

No, Dad, it isn't. It isn't all right.

He walks me to the locker room. It is empty except for us. We talk of winning and losing, of dreaming and trying. He says that winning isn't the point.

For when that one great scorer comes,
To mark against your name.
'Tis not whether you won or lost,
But how you played the game.

"The important thing is you did your best," he says.

We talk of many things—how well I ran, how surprised the crowd was to see their favorite track stars losing to a football player. He tells me that I can do anything in life, with my life, that I dream I can. He tells me many things. But he doesn't tell me the truth. Surely he knows. . . .

I didn't do my best. I quit. I quit to show you. To show you my pain, my need to fail. To not be everything that you expect me to be. To show you that I don't deserve the crown you are passing. To show you I want out. I quit the moment I could taste victory because winning is what I have always done. I am seen as a winner; I feel at a loss. Did you love my Mother? Was I born out of love and joy in the hope and dream of happiness? Were you, the two of you, ever happy? Was there a time when it wasn't complicated?

I hope that he will recognize how deep my pain, my fear. I pray that he will ask, "Why did you quit? Why did you not do your best?" so that I can spill my heart, my soul, my guts. That both he and I might have a chance to survive and go our separate ways. Together.

But he never asked. He told me many things. Wise, wonderful, beautiful, encouraging things. But he never asked . . . and I never told him . . . the truth.

The truth would come in an August death, and this was but early May.

Peter falls backward. The fetal Hoover dangles in his hand. Toni looks expectantly at him. Was that thwack the sound of a baby being suctioned from the womb? I wrench myself back into this moment, this decade, to tell Toni what she cannot see. The gadget came loose from the baby's head. My God, I think, how can a fragile, almost newborn baby withstand all this yanking and pushing and pressing and pulling?

And when does it end, the yanking and pushing and pressing and pulling? When are children allowed to be?

I glance at the fetal monitor. Our child's pulse is steady and normal, humming right along at 156 beats per minute. The heart of a long-distance runner?

Peter reaches over and turns a knob on the Hoover. I don't have to be told what this means. He has increased the force of the suction. Oh, no. How can the head of a tiny unborn child withstand all this? He tells Toni they are going to try it again. Not long to wait. The contractions are less than a minute apart. Here we go again.

He slides the Hoover up inside Toni. She pushes. Her veins pop. Jackie coaches, the pregnant doctor presses, and Peter pulls. And pulls. And *pulls!* I'm crazed with anxiety. Why isn't the baby coming? I want to scream. Stop. Stop this! It is too much. I can't stand it!

Thwwaacckk!

I catch the scream in my throat seconds before it fills the delivery room with my horror. I gasp for air in relief as I see there is no baby's head dangling at the bloody end of the Hoover where it was pulled from the fragile body still inside Toni. . . .

Thwwaacckk!

The sound of shattered glass brings me out of my rage. I stop pounding the side of the garage and follow the sound to its source. The huge Douglas fir in our backyard obscures my view of the back door. Out of a dream I remember him heading in that direction. I start for the back door. Before I get there, the screams start. I stop. I try to roll back time.

"Let's go fishing, Dad. I can stack hay tomorrow. Or never. But let's go fishing. Let's not do this. Not today. Not ever."

But it is too late. The screams, so long held silent, are finding their voice. Their voices, for we are all in it. Family violence will give full voice to the scream so long stuck in the discord of family silence.

The voice I hear is my Sister's. She is the first to scream. (And the last to know?) In slow motion I reach to open the back door. My hand slips on the bloody doorknob. I am transfixed by the blood on my hand. It has come from the blood that has dripped from the shattered window above, where my Father cut himself as he broke and entered. I touch it. Our blood mingles. It is the same color as my own, which oozes from knuckles bared to bone on the wall of the garage. But I do not scream. My turn is yet to come.

My Father has left his blood behind and he is way ahead of me, but I know his plan. . . .

Break and enter. Search and destroy.

My Mother screams.

I push open the door, enter, and move up the steps into the kitchen. Why can't I get there faster? Am I doing my best? The untended undergrowth of familial weeds has grown flammable beyond imagining and needs only the spark of my Father's rage to ignite and burn beyond control. I can no longer be the happy smile and cool rain that dampen the fires of dysfunction. I cannot diffuse the violence, for it is already exploding. All around me.

The first scream fades as my Sister runs out the front door, seeking sanctity wherever she can find it. At the neighbor's house. Wherever she can find it. Has she found it?

> *My Father's spirit in arms! All is not well.*
> *I doubt some foul play. Would the night were*
>   *come!*
> *Till then sit still my soul. Foul deeds will rise,*
> *Though all the earth o'erwhelm them, to men's*
>   *eyes.*

The screams of my Mother grow muffled. . . .

The Hoover hangs ineffectually in Peter's hand. He is surprised that this baby will not move. It seems so ready to and yet. . . . Toni and I are left in limbo as Peter and the pregnant doctor have a quick confab in medical lingo. I can't understand what in the hell they are saying. It is out of my hands. I am being taught something, being forced to let go, to trust strangers. I should be pleased: I've got two doctors for the price of one, a Warren Beatty look-alike and a woman with child. I would count my blessings but there isn't time. Another contraction. Oh, no . . . Peter reaches for the knob on the Hoover. Gives it a turn. I'm desperate to say something, to interfere.

Stay out of the way. Let go.

I hesitate. Too late. The moment is gone. Contraction. Pushing, pulling, pressing, coaching. I am swept away in a cacophony of sound. If I had become the composer I dreamed of being during my college days, I would attempt a symphony. "The Rites of Birth."

The Rites of Death.

It is the most intensely human mixture of totally unselfconscious sound I have ever heard. Except one.

The rattle of death.

My prayers for deliverance are a part of the cacophonous symphony:
Deliver me my baby. Peter pulls.
Deliver me from my Father's ghost. Toni pushes.
Deliver me from my life of regret. My Father pushes.
Deliver me. . . .
Thwwwaaaaccckkk!

Chapter Nineteen

*T*hwack!. . . the starter's pistol fires.
Thwwaacckk!. . . the 12-gauge shotgun explodes
past the left ear of my twelve-year-old head.
Thwwwaaaccckkk!

I come through the kitchen into the living room. My Mother's muffled cries come from her bedroom. I turn to see my Brother. He stands in the hallway with his .243 Winchester Savage raised and ready. It points where I cannot see, down the hallway to her bedroom. Does he know I am there? Do I? I am out of the way and I cannot see everything. I take a step toward the hallway. To do what? Repair the broken window? Wipe the blood from my Father's hands? Wipe the moment clean? Save my Mother from what has already happened?

Someone comes running out of the tumult. I step back.

A pajama-clad figure, its face disfigured, puffy, and blue, comes stumbling around the corner of the hallway door. I step further back. Out of the way. The abused figure lurches past me, out of the dying room and into the living room. A dreamy recognition creeps into my daze. It is my Mother. Who else? I know this house, this family. I know who sleeps where, from whose bedroom she has escaped. Hers. Theirs? But bedrooms are for the consummation of life, not death. Did they know, as they slept in marital bliss, that marital murder was the real child of their conjugal bed?

I know something is happening here that has been going to happen for decades. This is the moment I have dreamed of in all my childhood nightmares. I have spent my youth pricking the bubble of violence as it grew, but it has grown nonetheless. I want it to stop. I know not how. Where to start. Console my Mother, disarm my Brother, protect my Father . . . save my Self? I stand rooted in the impossible options of my cowardice.

"Put down the gun."

It is my Father's voice. The .243 Winchester Savage remains level, my Brother's cheek nestled to its stock, his eye glued to its sights.

"Put down the gun," says my Father again and closer.

I cannot see, but I know he has taken a step. Closer. Too close.

Thwwwaaaccckkk!

I jump out of my skin. Out of my life. The .243 Winchester has savagely spoken and my Father has taken his last step, and then, unbelievably, says his last words, "Oh, my God. . . ."

Thump! His body hits the floor. My Brother has not missed. I am out of the way and I cannot see, but I know he has not missed. I take a step.

"Get out of here," says my Brother, who has been the best Big Brother I could ever want. Who has defended me against the world, even against my Father. Who was the first-born and bore the greatest burden of our Father's constant pushing. Who was never given what innately should have been his, or any child's—respect for his uniqueness. Who was never accepted for what he was, but always and continually chastised for what he wasn't. Who was lectured and goaded and made to eat with the dog.

"Get out of here," says my Big Brother, who has let his irksome Little Brother tag along to explore his Big Brother world for as long as I can remember, and the .243 Savage swings in my direction and I no longer want to tag along. I despise myself for the fear that rushes through me. How can I be afraid when my Mother has been beaten, my Father killed, my Sister terrorized and still running, and my Brother burdened with the horror of doing what he could not help? How could I fear for my life when everything else has been already lost?

I take the first step backwards of thousands I will take in my life in moments of crisis. I step backwards. I will never run the same way again. I go on the defensive. Let others pull the trigger, score the touchdowns, push the moment to its crisis. I step backwards and away.

I stumble into the front room. My Mother is a huddled figure on the window seat. I go to her. Her face is beaten beyond recognition. But I recognize her. And her terror.

Did she not see it coming? Did she sleep soundly this beautiful Sunday morning? How could she not know that tragedy was just around the corner? And needed only a final nudge. I go to her but I cannot console her, for I have gone somewhere else.

My Father lies in a heap on the bedroom floor; his blood spatters the wallpaper with proof of the violence that has slept there so many years; my Sister sobs down the street where she has run; my Brother picks up the phone to call for justice (is there such a thing?); and I have gone somewhere else, very far away and silent and within.

I look out the big bay windows toward the Castle Mountains, where I have hunted and played and spent my youth. Time passes, but I know not that it has for I am out of the way and have gone somewhere else.

Two men carry a stretcher through the front room. I turn from the fireplace mantel, where I have been standing in close examination of the Charles M. Russell bronzes that my Father bought because he loved beautiful things. His shoes stick out from under the sheet. There is a hole in his sole. A hole in the soul to match the hole in his heart. The hole in me. The well-worn shoes of his worn-out life pass before my eyes, through the front room, and out the front door.

That it should come to this. . . .

I don't know where anyone is, for I have gone somewhere far away. They try to find me. But they never will.

I sit in the backyard in the front seat of his car. Not a Jaguar XK140 Roadster but a used 1959 Volkswagon and a far, far cry from the beauty and elegance of his life's dream. They come to me and ask if I am all right. I cannot understand the question. A cup of water is handed to me. I take it. Then pills. I take them. This gets me what I want and they all go away. I look in the backseat and see his suitcase, his briefcase, a manuscript of the book he was writing—"The Great Dilemma: Or How to Free Man In Spite of Himself"—his life's possessions. And now will they take this, too?

"How to free man in spite of himself...." I don't think this is what he had in mind.

Three hundred dollars, a 1959 Volkswagon, a suitcase of clothes, and life. He had it all. But now it is all gone. And I have gone, too. Far, far away, where it will be safe. Where I can be whatever it is I am to be. But I do not know what that is.

I never want to get out of the 1959 Volkswagon. I don't remember that I did.

Thwwwaaaccckkk!

I am yanked out of the 1959 Volkswagon. The fetal Hoover has come loose, yet again, from the baby's head. Peter is telling Toni the good news and the bad. I eavesdrop from my helpless position of honor on Toni's right. Good news. The baby's head has moved. Bad news. Not enough.

Peter tells Toni he is going to use forceps to move the baby's head into the birth canal. Toni is gasping for air.

The doctor glances at me....

My Brother turns toward me....

The forceps are handed to him.

The .243 Winchester Savage swings in my direction.

The forceps look like instruments of torture from a dungeon of long ago.

Of not so long ago.

Cold steel . . .

Hot lead . . .

About to touch the tender, malleable head of our child.

That has rent my heart, my Father's heart, in two. . . .

I crumble inside.

I run into the front room, into my Self. . . .

I see there is no other choice. I nod at Peter.

I see there was no other choice. . . .

From a natural birth at home to forceps in a hospital. It has been a long journey.

From the death of my Father to the birth of my child.

Getting ready for what has been coming for forty-five hours.

For forty-three years. . . .

Peter warns Toni that the forceps will feel very strange, very foreign, and not to be frightened. He slides them inside her. She takes it like a woman. The contraction comes. . . . Push. Press. Finesse. Peter eases the handles of the forceps back toward him. Delicate touch. Oh, to be so young, handsome, and accomplished! It makes the void of expertise in my life glaring. Jack-of-all-trades, expert at none. But this man knows what he is doing. Peter smiles. The baby's head has moved! It is engaged in the birth canal. Six inches separate it from what we call life.

Time to make the immortal mortal. Time to bring this baby home. Into our arms. Into life.

Peter tells Toni she must give it everything she has. Hasn't she always? She gathers herself. Jackie cheers her on. The pregnant doctor puts all her weight on Toni's belly. Push, push, push. Veins bulge. Toni's entire upper body goes red. Slowly, the baby descends. Down two inches, back one, down two, back one. At last . . . the baby's head can be seen in the vaginal opening. Crowning they call it. Two contractions come and go. The head will not pass. Toni and I know what is coming. Episiotomy. Alas, but this child has inherited my hat size. The perineum must be cut to make room for the large head. Peter gives Toni a local anesthetic, the only drug she has had during the entire pregnancy and birth. He cuts her perineum. Here comes the contraction.

What will be, will be. Mortality awaits and . . . it's a boy! George William Benedict Niewoehner slides effortlessly into the world at 8:22 p.m., February 28, 1988.

What will be, will be. Immortality awaits. George Edward Niewoehner is borne effortlessly into that "other" world . . . "the undiscovered country" at 8:22 p.m., February 28, 1988. I feel him go. It is I who have kept him here and I feel him go. On March 13, 1912, he began his mortal journey. His cesarean death was August 4, 1963. He has waited twenty-five years for this moment—a mere speck in the ocean of infinity, but a lifetime for me in my finite world of anguish and pain.

I see the profound wisdom in my Father's admonishment that we always die by our own hands. Nobody kills us but ourselves. When we are born we greet the enemy, and he is us. Not our parents; not our teachers, bosses, and loved ones; not cancer, heart disease and war; not our first-born son . . . but us!

My Father died by his own hand.

The death we choose is a reflection of the life we have lived. He chose the moment; he chose the means.

The ghost of my Father is no longer in the room, no longer in my mortal thoughts. I hear his good-bye in the cry of his Grandson and . . . he is gone.

I have seen it all: the death of a Father, the birth of a son.

Peter lays George William Benedict Niewoehner on Toni's belly. Our eyes meet. Our souls touch. There is no need for words.

I am handed a pair of scissors with which to cut the cord. The gristle-like quality of it astonishes me. It is extremely difficult to cut. How strong is our connection to the Universe! A surge of animal instinct prompts me to bite through it with my teeth. I bear down on the scissors.

You asked for it, son. Say good-bye to infinity. There is no turning back . . . snip! Welcome to the world.

George takes his first breath of finity. A bright pink glow replaces the waxy, pale-gray hue of his skin. It starts in his chest (the heart) and spreads with each succeeding breath to his hands and feet. He has just gone through billions of years of evolution. From the ocean of the womb to the air of the world. His journey has begun.

Toni and I laugh at the size of his rib cage as he hungrily drinks in the air.

"Your head and your chest," she says.

"Let's just hope he has your temperament," I say. She agrees. I married an honest woman.

February 28, 1988, 8:22 p.m. George William Benedict Niewoehner's numerological, astrological charts are loaded. As it is a leap year, he has missed February 29 by three and one-half hours. Missed my own birth date of March 1 by just over a day.

"Of all the women whose babies I have delivered, you are the best," Peter tells Toni. "I've never seen anything like it." Toni smiles. How little he knows how right he is.

No one can believe how beautiful and rested she looks. You would never suspect the journey this woman took to have her baby on her own terms—the old-fashioned way.

Peter turns to me, holds out his hand. "We aren't so horrible after all, are we? Us doctor-types?" I laugh. Take his hand and babble hopelessly inadequate words of gratitude. He shrugs.

It would take hours to explain how it all came to be. That it all began years ago. With the death of my Father, the birth of his ghost. The search within my Self for peace.

Toni and I got the experience we deserved, the child we deserved. He was born exactly as he was meant to be born and will show us, as he already has, the truth about ourselves. He chose us. We are the cross he was meant to bear.

And he will die, as we all do, by his own hand.

Chapter Twenty

Georage William," I say to my Mother from the pay phone down the hall from the delivery room. I know she's pleased to hear we named him after Dad, but she covers it with concern over which last name will be on the birth certificate.

"Both . . . Benedict and Niewoehner. When he gets older he can use whichever one he likes best. Or make up his own."

"Seven pounds, four ounces. Lots of hair. Olive skin."

"Toni's fine."

"I'm fine. . . ."

My Father's name hangs in the air. As it has for twenty-five years. We skirt around it. As we have for twenty-five years. I want to tell her it's all right.

It's all right. I am free at last. He is gone. All is forgiven. We are all forgiven. Him, too. He understands. He is gone. We can go on living without skirting around the edges. I love you. I love my Brother. I love my Sister. Let us be whole again.

I want to tell her. We say good-bye instead. I hang up the phone. Maybe I'll write a book. Tell the world. Word will get around. . . .

The only secrets we keep are those we are ashamed of. I have no shame. Nor should any of us. I have only an open heart, infinite gratitude . . . and love.

I go out the front door of the hospital. I have left Toni and George nestled in each other's arms. I want to howl at the moon, tell the world. . . .

I look up at the moon outside Cedars Sinai. Impossible to imagine this is the same moon of yesterday, yester-life, when Toni and I took our stroll through hard labor and Agua Dulce fruit trees. I glance around. No ghosts. I cross the wet streets to a cozy bar that is tucked next to the Hard Rock Cafe.

The double shot of twenty-five-year-old McCallan's scotch seems nectar from Never Never Land. It hits a stomach that hasn't had food for days, a mind that hasn't slept in *ages*, and a soul that hasn't cried for*ever*. This could be the start of something new.

I walk quickly out of the bar and into the drizzle. Out of the rain and under an awning. Out of the past and into the future. Out of the agony and into . . .

The tingle starts in my heart. With each pump it spreads to my emotional nether regions. Orgasmically it comes. Closer and closer. My heart is pounding. I lean against the side of the Hard Rock Cafe. Closer and closer. I can't catch my breath. The rain is coming harder now. The drought is over. Harder and closer, and I can't breathe, but I can do what I have not done, and the cry I hear is my own. The drought is over and the tears come in surging orgasms of emotion.

I cry for all the heartache and pain that I have had and caused. I cry because I never went fishing, because I could not run as I once did, because I could not love as I wanted, because I was not the son I tried to be. I cry because now I am the Father, the Husband, and now it is up to me. I cry because I am human. And it is not my fault.

I cry because I am free.

Epilogue

D addy, I want to tell you something." When George starts a conversation like this I know he means business. I put down my spoonful of oatmeal. He pushes his miso soup to the side and pins me with deep brown eyes that are light years wiser than his four years. "We should go fishing."

My heart leaps.

"You are absolutely right, George. And we will."

"Soon!" he says, gesturing emphatically with his hand. "But not dolphins. Cause they're our friends."

"How 'bout trout?" I suggest.

"Are they faster than sharks?" he asks, being Piscean and besotted with anything that inhabits the sea.

"Faster. And more fun to catch."

"When?" he asks, not letting me off the hook.

"Tomorrow."

And tomorrow came, and then we went fishing.